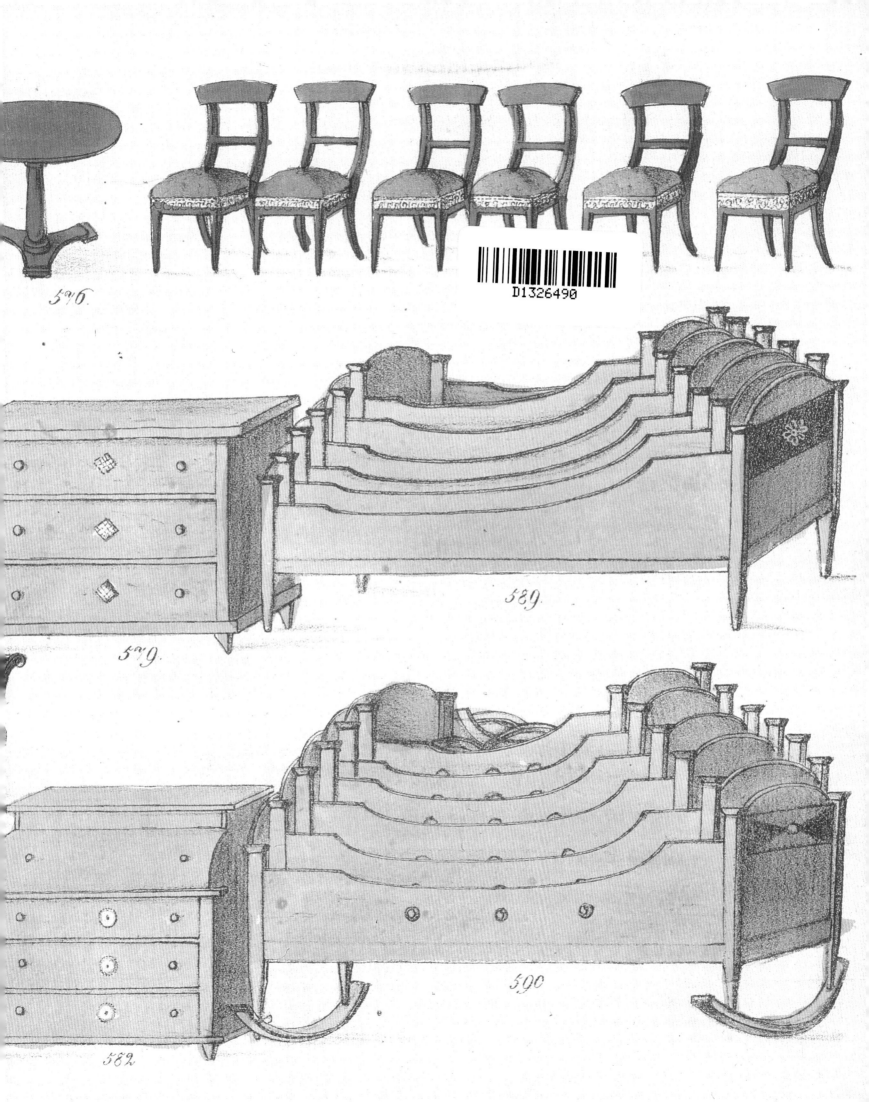

576.

579.

582.

589.

590.

DOLLS'
HOUSES

DOLLS' HOUSES

Domestic life and architectural styles in miniature
from the 17th century to the present day

OLIVIA BRISTOL AND
LESLIE GEDDES-BROWN

MITCHELL BEAZLEY

ENDPAPERS
Details from the toy catalogues dating from 1840 by the German Lindner firm.

PAGE 1
Rock & Gräner's fantasy French style bed dating from c.1850.

PAGE 2
A little girl with her neat white apron, is pictured in this oil painting of around 1870, creating her own make-believe house in an old cupboard with curtains. A small toy horse and cart is beside her.

PAGE 3
Boston house with mansard roof c.1880.

PAGE 5
German bureau c.1870 with real drawers. Knole settee from the Stockbroker Tudor period.

DOLLS' HOUSES
by Olivia Bristol and Leslie Geddes-Brown

First published in Great Britain in 1997 by Mitchell Beazley
an imprint of Reed International Books Limited
Michelin House, 81 Fulham Road, London SW3 6RB
and Auckland and Melbourne

Executive Editor Alison Starling
Executive Art Editor Vivienne Brar
Editor Nina Sharman
Designer Lisa Tai
Picture Research Wendy Gay
Production Jilly Sitford

Special photography Tim Ridley, Tim Knox, Steve Tanner and Ian Booth

The publishers will be grateful for any information which will assist them in keeping future editions up to date. Although all reasonable care has been taken in the preparation of this book, neither the publishers nor the compilers can accept any liability for any consequence arising from the use thereof or the information contained herein.

A CIP record for this book is available from the British Library

ISBN 1 85732 824 8

Set in Goudy and Grotesque
Printed and bound in China

Contents

Introduction

Traditionally historians have never cared overmuch about children, their lives and their playthings. Politics, wars and treaties were what mattered. So we know much less about how children played than how they were exploited by, say, slavery or big business. We see them in 17th-century portraits clutching stiff little dolls and in 18th-century equivalents romping with hoops and tops as well as dogs, cats and parrots, and contemporary paintings are some of the best evidence we have of what their lives were really like. Of course, as the paintings are only of the great and good, little survives to tell us about the daily life of poorer children.

Further back in time, archaeologists have dug up pieces of miniature furniture and crockery which might well have been part of a dolls' house, but, lacking any evidence of the house itself, the experts have tended to think these tiny objects were somehow devotional. But, in many cases, there's no evidence for that either. What is certain is that household objects, carefully made in miniature, go back to Ancient Egypt; others have been found which date from the days of Classical Greece and Ancient Rome. When, after the Blitz, archaeologists dug in the oldest areas of London, they found a tiny Roman wine jug of the first century AD, a miniature medieval bronze cauldron and a green-glazed earthenware jug dating from the second half of the 14th century. These were faithful copies of fashionable contemporary crockery – another good way of dating them. More recently an exhibition of metal toys, many collected from the Thames in London over the last 20 years, has suggested that toys were being mass-produced as early as 1300. These include cooking equipment and furniture, some of which seems designed to fit on walls. There are also a series of "fish on grill" toys which copy similar Roman toys. The collector, Geoff Egan, believes there were early dolls' houses too but not being made of metal, they have not survived.

No dolls' houses of any kind are known about in any form whatsoever before the mid-16th century, although discoveries are still being made. The great dolls' house historian, Flora Gill Jacobs, records how the discovery of a miniature rocking chair in a London plague pit forced the antiquarian, Carl Depperd, to recant his view that America had invented the rocker. The evidence was irrefutable. The chair, 9cm (3½in) high, was clearly made in the reign of Charles I since other items in the plague pit testified the date. The chair was miraculously preserved in its hideous grave. "Even the little seat cushion of

△ A little German doll with brown hair (this is rare: they are usually fair or dark). She is a china-head dating from the 1860s. Her heavy top and skirt are contemporary, although home-made.

▷ Christian Hacker mansard-roofed house, c.1880, from the Musée des Arts Decoratifs, Paris. Although French in style and made in Germany, these houses were exported to Britain, France and the United States.

this toy rocker was intact," said Depperd. "This tiny toy is a new starting point in rocking-chair research." New evidence may still be found to prove that dolls' houses were toys for children in Ancient Egypt, Assyria or even that most dismal of times, the Dark Ages.

THE FIRST DOLLS' HOUSE

To date, the first real evidence we have is the commission, by Albrecht V, Duke of Bavaria, of a dolls' house for his daughter in 1558. He probably thought this a minor part of his life but because of the importance of the dolls' house, he is better known for this action than anything else. He was obviously very pleased with the result, for he put the house in his art collection and, presumably, rarely allowed the little girl to play with it. The story would have ended there, since the grand miniature house seems to have been burnt in the fire at the

ducal palace in 1674, except that in 1598 both it and its contents were carefully inventoried.

We thus know that it was four storeys high, we know the names of the court box-maker, locksmiths and painter who were put to work on the project (their bills still exist) and we know, more or less, where the rooms were. The lower floor was given over to the stables, cow shed, coach house, wine cellar and larder along with the office (it was quite common to have integral animal sheds at this period); next came the ground floor with the kitchen and, outside, a garden and orchard. The next floor up was the grandest of all and included a ballroom where the Duke and Duchess were looked after by six servants

▷ The design of this strange little set of furniture can be dated exactly because of its box, which shows the Chicago World's Fair of 1893, where it was first exhibited. It is made of soft alloy, described as "indestructible". There are velvet drop-in seats and ribbons twined in the filigree metal backs.

△ Germany cornered the 19th-century toy market. This Biedermeier style set continued to be made long after the fashion ended.

and where their table was, again typically for the period, covered by a rich carpet, probably from the Orient. There were musical instruments on the table and, on a side table, gold and silver dishes. Next door was a handy bedroom with tapestry-lined walls and a fabric-hung bed.

The top floor had a chapel (integral chapels were often built into grand houses) with a priest and band of musicians. Beside it – perhaps indicating how unimportant the chapel really was – seems to have been a box room stuffed with at least three beds plus chests and chairs. The floor also held the nurseries, a work room for spinning and sewing and a second kitchen. This was the best kitchen, home of the good silver, and probably where the ladies had informal meals.

Another record of the house adds that there was also a room to store the armour (great families would be able to call on the services of small armies when necessary) and, more extraordinarily, a lion house. The lion was the heraldic insignia of the Dukes of Bavaria. Although it was greatly admired at the time, there is no suggestion that Duke Albrecht's house was a novel idea. Such a magnificent object as this dolls' house with its chapel and stable, bed hangings and tapestries is most unlikely to have been the first ever made. Its magnificence, indeed, suggests that it was one of the greatest ever created, the descendant of many less palatial dolls' homes reaching back into history.

Thus the history of dolls' houses starts abruptly in mid-16th century Germany and continues there, and in the Low Countries, for the next century. English dolls' houses appeared in the very early 18th century and American ones in the late 18th century; the Mediterranean countries seem to have had less of a passion for dolls' houses, although examples are found.

A CHILD'S LOT

The mid-16th century was a time of revival for Europe as the Renaissance, which started in 14th-century Italy, gathered power and moved through the continent. Such great thinkers as Erasmus, John Calvin and Martin Luther, artists such as

▽ Celluloid was invented earlier than we think. This little German doll has hair like a Gibson Girl and dates from around the 1890s. Is she a clown from a circus or does her jester's cap and short flounced skirt mean she's going to a fancy-dress party?

▷ This American dolls' house is named Ramshackel Inn on the gable after the title of a play. It was given to the comedienne Zasu Pitts in about 1905 when she was young. Later in life she added pictures of herself in her best-loved roles. The furniture also covers several decades. It is very much in the turn-of-the-19th-century opulent style.

◁ Clever designers created dolls' houses that could be assembled from flat board. This room set, by McLoughlin Bros of New York, has intricately printed details of the interior. Note the heavy wallpaper border and ornate overmantel with stag's head.

Benvenuto Cellini and Andrea Palladio, and "Renaissance men" with many gifts – Philip Sidney, Walter Raleigh and Thomas Wyatt – had been born towards the start of the century. The second half saw the births of William Shakespeare, Francis Bacon and Ben Jonson in England, and Peter Paul Rubens, Frans Hals and Anthony van Dyck on the continent. It was a time of great men and, with Elizabeth I and Catherine de Medici ruling England and France, of great women too.

Children, however, were yet to have a renaissance of their own. But their condition was not as regimented as the portraits of the time might suggest. For a start, they were painted wearing their best clothes and on their best behaviour. Elizabeth Godfrey in her book, *Home Life under the Stuarts*, says that normally children wore plain overalls. She unearthed a tailor's bill for six holland coats, which cost a guinea to make. We do not know at this period whether children had their own dolls'

houses as playthings – those which survive are intended either for adults or, at best, to allow children to gaze but not play. But children did have dolls, for these do appear in the portraits. Lady Arabella Stuart, for instance, is painted dressed to the nines, with jewelled cap and bodice so embroidered that it looks stiff with a doll in her arms, dressed equally stiffly.

There were no printed storybooks as yet. Printing had been invented but was too expensive to lavish on children. Tales and nursery rhymes were handed down from generation to generation by families. Dolls, along with balls, whips, tops and hobby horses go back into the mists of time. St Bartholomew's Fair, established in 1133, had toy stalls along with sweets and dolls, which is why dolls were once called Bartholomew Babies. There were toy animals, too, such as lambs with white wool spangled in gold, composition heads with reddened cheeks, pert black eyes and pink ribbons around their necks.

FAMOUS OWNERS

Dolls' houses, too, have always attracted royalty, perhaps because the nobility have so little chance to play house themselves. Queen Anne was a dolls' house enthusiast who gave a brilliant example to her goddaughter, Ann Sharp, which is still in existence (see pages 38–9). A more unlikely enthusiast for dolls' houses is the Russian Tsar, Peter the Great. He is thought to have become so excited by a dolls' house he saw as a young man on a visit to Holland that, on gaining the throne, he commissioned one for himself. This took five years to complete at a cost of 20,000 florin and Peter, in a fit of penury, turned it down as too expensive. Academics are still speculating if it exists and if so which Dutch house it is.

Queen Victoria's passion for her rather undistinguished house is well known; better still is the extraordinary creation made by the British people for Queen Mary (all sorts of experts were called in from Lutyens to J. M. Barrie) – although this is more of a scale miniature than a dolls' house. It did, however, rouse American prohibitionists to ire because of its wine cellar.

Dolls were also to be found in the White House. In 1878, 10-year-old Fanny Hayes, daughter of President Rutherford B. Hayes, was presented with a carpenter-made house at a Methodist fair in Baltimore (see also page 103). The house was lost and forgotten until the wife of the great grandson of the President restored it to its former glory in 1959. Sadly, however, an actual copy of the White House, made for the children of President Grover Cleveland, has so far vanished without trace. Alice Roosevelt, daughter of President Theodore Roosevelt, also had a dolls' house – but played with it before the family gained the White House. This house has also been revived and restored.

COLLECTING

Collecting dolls' houses, whether it be a replica of a real house, a cabinet or a cupboard house, has an equally long pedigree, although there are vastly more adult collectors today than even 50 years ago. As long ago as the 18th century, women were collecting dolls' houses (there are few male collectors) as

◁ A late example of a carpenter-made dolls' house. The house was made in neo-Tudor style for seven-year-old Helen Worthington by Lord Warwick's estate carpenter in 1916. The hanging centre lights are wired for electricity.

opposed to commissioning their own. Sara Ploos van Amstel, the wife of a wealthy Dutch merchant, bought three old dolls' houses in an auction of 1743 and set about creating one of her own from the pieces (see page 52). Since then, collectors have been fascinated by the miniature worlds created by others and, although the chances of buying or finding an unknown 17th- or early 18th-century house are extremely remote and those which come on the market are the preserve of the rich, there is a constant stream of both mass-produced and hand-made 19th- and 20th-century houses for sale, with new, interesting versions still turning up from nowhere.

△ Very much in the Heidi gemütlich style, this bob-haired little girl with rick-rack decorated dress came from the Lord Roberts Workshops c.1920. Made of wood, the limbs are jointed.

▽ Little black dolls were also made for dolls' houses. This German doll dates from c.1920. She is smartly dressed in approved middle-class mode.

△ A very rare example of a British Raj dolls' house designed by a father (Mr Daddy) stationed in the East. Its towers slide into grooves and can be removed, making it easier to transport. The windows are charmingly pierced in the oriental style.

Dolls' houses appeal to adults and children alike and over the years an obsession with them has been handed down from generation to generation. In the second half of the 19th century there was an ever-increasing middle class interested in dolls' houses and that market had to be catered for. From the mid-19th century onwards dolls' houses were mass-produced by Britain, Germany and the United States. In Britain, Silber & Fleming (as distributors) and G. & J. Lines Ltd (as makers), both based in London, were the main firms. Christian Hacker and Moritz Gottschalk are among the most famous German manufacturers, and Rufus Bliss (see pages 128–9) and Converse are probably the most well-known American makers. The mass-production of dolls' houses from the mid-19th century satisfied the market at the time and many of these are still available today.

Just as surprise finds of antiquities and Chippendale furniture are still turning up in old attics and cupboards, historical dolls' houses are also appearing. Who knows, for instance, what may come from Eastern European and Baltic cupboards or from the storehouse of American attics? Similarly, dolls and their miniature furniture are also being re-discovered and re-attributed. Our *fin-de-siècle* interest in social history, rather than political or military actions, is at last revealing basic and important facts about the way children (and their parents) have always played.

A late 17th-century Swedish dolls' house mirrors the real 17th-century houses of Stockholm, with roof detail, soft stone and grey paintwork and characteristic close-set windows.

CHAPTER ONE

17th-Century Cabinet Houses

In the age of discovery, when other continents seemed as exotic as other worlds, people began to make miniature houses. These early houses from Germany and Holland were made for two different reasons – part vehicle of household instruction and part collector's cabinet. The objects were made by the finest craftsmen and artists and they are superb in detail. These baby and cabinet houses bring domestic history to life and tell us a great deal about life in Northern Europe at that time.

◁ The earliest known dolls' house dates from 1611 and comes from Nuremberg, Germany. It stands 2.7m (9ft) high. Over a cellar basement is a formal garden with gallery beside the great hall. The kitchen, surprisingly, is a floor above alongside an extremely formal drawing room (with later furniture). The walls and ceilings are decorated with swags and rosettes as well as mirrors, pewter and china on walls and shelves.

▷ The great hall of the 1611 house features a detailed mural showing a rather *risqué* picnic. There is a small orchestra, dancing couples and others sat around a table fondling each other. Their dress is contemporary with the house, as is the painted garden behind.

Until saleroom prices for teddy bears, dolls and dolls' houses astounded all but the most avid collectors, nobody except a few enthusiasts gave much thought to toys and their place in history. Their past went unrecorded, their fabric was allowed to decay. As recently as 1977, the collector Constance Eileen King writes of finding Ann Sharp's famous and important dolls' house, the earliest known in Britain and the gift of Queen Anne to her god-daughter, in a sorrowful state.

Although in "the care" of a museum, this singular record of life in 18th-century England was without its furniture, which was stored in boxes. It was, she said, like "visiting the burned-out shell of a once-loved home." She added that it was, "saddening to be made aware of the casualness with which some museums still regard playthings of the past, even, as in this case, when the importance is known."

This neglect has since been rectified and our attitude to toys has taken on a new seriousness but, like many of the great houses and works of art they copied, dolls' houses over the years have been neglected, ill-treated and even destroyed. Their unique contribution to how life was lived as long as 400 years ago has been little studied.

The first actual dolls' house still in existence dates from 1611 and depicts a three-storey Nuremberg town house (see left), for the city was already establishing its reputation as toy capital of the western world, one which it would keep until the 20th century and the First World War brought it to an end.

Although the contents of this 2.7m (9ft) high Nuremberg house were restored in the 18th century, it has many interesting features. Its heavy base is, naturally enough, the cellar but above is a charming garden, just the sort of enclosed space a townhouse would have, with balustraded galleries and plants climbing up the stone walls. Next door is the great hall (see above), with a "tapestry" painted around its walls showing a riotous picnic taking place in just such a garden. Couples are dancing to stringed instruments, there is a jester and a long, damask covered table, and a lot of kissing and cuddling is taking place. In the distance, in a neat parterre, children are playing with their pet dog. This may be the same dog that is depicted lying in the great hall under the mural. The adult nature of the scene suggests that this was not a toy for children.

On the next floor there is one of those extraordinarily busy kitchens for which these early houses are famed. The houses were used to teach young girls the rudiments of housekeeping, which is strange since families able to afford such richly appointed cabinets were also able to afford servants. But, Anna Koferlin, a German spinster keen on education, created a dolls' house in 1631 with that very intention.

△ Early dolls' houses could be simple. This one from Nuremberg consists of two rooms only and dates from the later 17th century. The kitchen full of implements and corner stove is typical of the period.

Anna Koferlin was one of the first collectors to put her dolls' house on view to the public, for a fee. Her house is no longer in existence but we have an idea of what it was like from a woodcut on the cover of a booklet that she wrote. She claims in the booklet that children will see, from the toy, how a household should be properly run. In 1765 Paul von Stetten writes: "As to the education of girls, I must make mention of the toys with which many played until they became brides... so-called dolls' houses. In these everything which belonged to a house and its management was reproduced in little and many went to such lengths of sumptuousness that the cost of such a plaything would run to 1,000 gulden and more." Although sumptuous these early houses belonged to merchants rather than aristocrats. The rich bourgeoisie were keen to keep up appearances and wanted their children to have every modern toy available.

THE TOY MAKERS

Although Nuremberg was a major toy centre, the toys were not made by toy specialists but by craftsmen skilled in cabinet making, silversmithing and pewter casting. Christoph Weigel, writing in 1698, refers to the guilds' work on toys: "The materials of which these dolls and playthings are made are in part silver and are fashioned by gold and silversmiths, in part of wood, which the common carver of images and turner are wont to make.... Others are moulded out of wax and in particular many kinds of beasts and fowls are made of this almost exactly like nature, with their rough skins drawn over them or very prettily bedecked with feathers. Indeed there is scarce a trade in which that which usually is made big may not often be seen copied on a small scale as a toy for playing with." The guilds were the trade unions of the 17th century and each artisan was strictly controlled. If a silversmith, for instance, wanted to add a wooden knop to a silver pot, he could not do it for himself but would have to apply to a knop maker.

Families were obviously very proud of their silver and pewter – and of the dolls' versions they ordered. The 1611 house (see page 15) shows the great hall with large pewter chargers above the tapestry and, in the kitchen, more are displayed on shelves from floor to ceiling. One reason for this – a common feature in dark Northern Europe – was that pewter, silver and glass all caught the flickers of candlelight and multiplied light levels. Lighting itself comes from brass chandeliers. These appear in the panelled drawing room with its white china wood stove, in the main bedroom and in the hall at the centre of the house.

A similar brass chandelier appears in the upper room of the two-room cupboard house (left) made in Germany during the second half of the 17th century. Because the scale is large, there is plenty of room for objects, plus a male doll sitting at a table covered with jugs and dishes and a female doll working beside the stove below. Like many of these early houses, the bedroom seems to double up as a sitting room (and, in this case, dining room too). The bed is piled high with duvets, the walls are panelled and, above, plates and finials are arranged in order.

By contrast, the Stromer house (right), with the date 1639 on its dormer window, has no less than 14 rooms, six of these rooms are large and busy, and include a kitchen positively glittering with pewter on its walls. Another eight rooms are crowded into the space of two large rooms and here there are horses stabled (with the stable lad's bed alongside), barrels of beer kept in storage, day and night nurseries with baby walker and rocking cradle, and rooms for storing dry goods and perishables. There is even a cage of chickens being fattened for the table. (Feather-covered birds were a speciality of Nuremberg and are often found in early dolls' houses.) This popular house gives a real feeling of life at the time.

▷ The Stromer house from Nuremberg dates from 1639. It is one of the most complete early houses, providing an amazing account of the interior of an affluent German home. The small rooms on either side of the grand entrance are divided into four and take in a cow byre, storage for beer and wine, dry goods and perishables, plus a nursery. The kitchen is typically on the first floor, like others of the period.

▽△ The kitchens of these early houses seem to be designed as much for the display of expensive pewter as for cooking. Typically the Stromer house has ranks of pewter on the walls and corner stove along with many implements from colanders to jelly moulds. Beside it is a grand hall and linen cupboard. The dining room (far right) has a green ceramic stove and pictures above the panelling. It is set out for entertaining.

Petronella Dunois (1650–95) was 26 and the daughter of an important official at the court of The Hague when she commissioned this dolls' house. A year later she married Pieter van Groenendijck, the Leiden regent and her dolls' house was listed as a major contribution to their household. It was handed down through the women of the family for 250 years until it was given to the Rijksmuseum in Amsterdam in 1934. An 18th-century inventory proves that many of the fittings are original. At one time the house was believed to have been made for Margaretha de Ruyter, who owned a similar cabinet house.

◁ Holland was at the height of her powers when these real houses were built in a style that swept the world. Rooms were full of light from the many-paned windows but houses were packed narrowly together with a final elegant gable to maximize space.

▽ The early Dutch houses are full of dolls, generally made of wax. This extraordinary fellow, found in the house's ground floor dining room, is a peasant dressed in the Waterland region style.

△ In a real house the cellar would have been underground. It is stocked with bottles of oil and jars of herbs; there are pies, chickens and a cow's head on the shelves while dried fish for winter hang on the walls. Little turned barrels of maple wood are for butter and beer. The buckets and jugs are made of silver.

DATE Made in 1676. The exact date and the initials PD are embroidered on a pincushion found in the miniature lying-in room.
SCALE 200cm (79in) high, 149cm (58½in) wide and 56cm (22in) deep.
STRUCTURE Typical Dutch marquetry cabinet of walnut veneered on oak standing on barley sugar twist legs and bun feet. Unlike other cabinets, however, each door has a central "window" to tease the viewer.
LAYOUT OF ROOMS In these early dolls' houses, the servants' rooms are at the top and consist of peat store, linen room and nursery. On the first floor are two big rooms, a chintz-hung lying-in room and a salon. On the ground floor is a "cellar" next to the kitchen and a dining room. The lowest ceilings are at the top and the highest on the *piano nobile*.

◁ The house is full of black-framed portraits of the late 16th century which, because they vary so in style, are probably copies of real paintings.

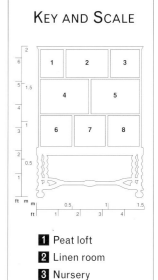

KEY AND SCALE

1 Peat loft
2 Linen room
3 Nursery
4 Lying-in room
5 Salon
6 Cellar
7 Kitchen
8 Dining room

Petronella Dunois

◁ Households in 17th-century Holland preferred peat to wood and stored it in large baskets in a peat loft. It was then delivered to different rooms in smaller containers. These willow baskets date from the 17th century and have the same patterns as you find today. This rough fellow could have come straight from a Breughel painting – he has a hump and a lewd expression while his coat and baggy trousers are of coarse linen. He may be one of the carriers who delivered the fuel to Dutch homes since he seems a bit macabre to be a household servant.

◁△ Laundry baskets have not changed much in 300 years. This version is made of woven willow in the traditional shape and with carrying handles at each end. Lids are less common today. It is somewhat out of proportion to the laundress. The laundry and basket are full of clothes – lace-trimmed caps and shirts, swaddling clothes used to wrap fractious babies and white wool blankets edged with blue silk.

▽ This stylish bed quilt has a coloured central pattern framed in buff cotton. Real versions would have been identical.

△ Japanese objects were all the rage when this dolls' house was made, for the country had only just been opened up to the West. This folding screen, in the Rimpa style, would have been the height of fashion and its asymmetric pattern looks so convincingly Japanese that it has probably been copied from an original.

◁ Nurseries were an important part of the 17th-century house – and equally important to the domesticated owners of dolls' houses (although Petronella Dunois never had any children). This nursery has an elaborate marbled fireplace and a fireguard made of silver. The bed, made of wood and card, is very grand with finials of silk and feathers a rare survival.

△ Within the cabinet house is a miniature cabinet made of oak and decorated with olive wood marquetry. The porcelain on the top is later, made at Meissen and painted with flowers, and the arrangement of different shapes is characteristic. The cabinet, which would have been kept locked, is filled with valuable, neatly folded linen placed on lace shelf covers.

▷ The spit in the kitchen is also of silver, perhaps because the metal is easily worked. It was used to roast meats by turning them before a fire. The spit is hallmarked with Michael Maenbeeck's mark.

ARCHITECTURAL CHARACTER

German dolls' houses from the 17th century are, mostly, very simple representations of real houses. They are heavy wooden cabinets divided into rooms, sometimes with a central staircase and sometimes with balustrading.

The Kress house, shown right and opposite, is another extraordinary survival from Nuremberg dating from the second half of the 17th century. Unlike the Stromer house (see pages 16–17), it is inhabited by dolls, although most of these were added in the 18th century. It is also architecturally more interesting. The two gables on the top are very fine, sharply peaked with flourishes where they meet the roof. There is a series of large rooms for the householders and small storage rooms and servants' hall in the basement. Each large room of this statuesque house has an arched proscenium with fine balusters opening onto the scene behind – very much as though each of these rooms is a separate stage. The effect is to enhance the action within – there is no feeling of exclusion.

The nursery in Kress house is at the top of the house where there is a very smart doll wearing a flower-embroidered dress and fichu carrying a tiny swaddled infant. These cruel bindings, similar to others found in toy nativities, were the 17th-century method of dealing with limbs bent by rickets (now known to be caused by a vitamin deficiency). In the same nursery an older baby doll sits in a high chair. The cupboards are stacked with neatly ironed linen and there is a sumptuous bed and counterpane.

In another top bedroom, another grand lady doll sits in her underclothes trying to decide what to wear that day – her choices are laid out, presumably by servants – while in the large kitchen, just as glittering with pewter as the Stromer house, a less grand-looking doll in commonplace clothes does the cooking. The kitchen is filled with jelly moulds, colanders, kettles and equipment for turning the spits, which are lined up above the stove.

Clearly, during this period the kitchen was the domain of the householder not the servants. (This was probably the case in real houses too.) In the Kress house it is sensibly placed opposite the dining room, where a man in a cocked hat (later in date) stands beside a ceramic stove near a set of beautifully embroidered high-backed chairs. In the dining room and the kitchen there is a fine display of blue-and-white pottery. The table, with complex ivory inlay, is covered with tankards, glasses and decanters, while the rustic table of the servants' hall below stairs has much coarser pewter ware and a huge beer jug. A painting of a horse adorns a door which leads to the stables where a model horse can be found along with a splendid studded saddle made of leather. At one side of the house, next to the servants' hall, is a tiny and simple bedroom, one

△ The series of small rooms on the ground floor need a complicated series of stairs to allow entry from the central hall. This was clearly the servants' section of the house.

▽ The kitchen, like all those of the period, is in the owners' part of the house, showing how important the area was. The massed ranks of implements and dishes were intended to show wealth as well as good housekeeping.

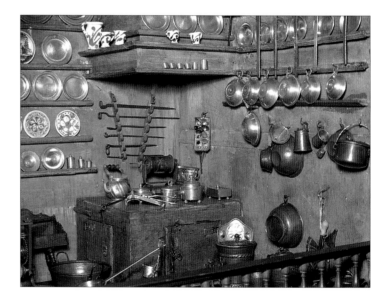

quarter the size of the owners' bedrooms, and directly opposite this there is a similar tiny bedroom, where a servant would have slept, guarding the room below, which is filled with barrels, wooden tubs and baskets of provisions.

The maker of the Kress house has even gone to the trouble of sorting out the complex arrangement of balconies, stairs and galleries whereby these smaller rooms could be reached from the rest of the house and, unlike other survivals of this period, the house still has its fine balusters.

▷ The Kress house from Nuremberg dates from the second half of the 17th century. The dolls were added in the 18th century. It takes its name from its previous owners, the Kress von Kressenstein family. Its narrowness and height, accentuated by fancy gables, are typical of real houses in Nuremberg. The dolls and furniture are kept in place by turned balustrades so it needs no exterior doors. Nonetheless, its architectural character is strong.

KITCHEN TECHNOLOGY

The problem of the over-equipped kitchen has been overcome in another early house, owned by a grand family from Ulm in Germany for about 400 years. Though the house itself may be later, the furniture and objects date from the 16th century. It, again, is stuffed with all sorts of kitchen equipment, but the kitchen itself takes up the space of two normal rooms. Pewter chargers cover the walls on built-in shelves that slope forwards so that the dishes would not gather dust on the front. Beautiful metal moulds for sweet and savoury jellies hang directly on the walls, there are rows of jugs from large to tiny, pans serried in ranks and a shelf-full of metal candlesticks.

The cooking arrangements seem to be the same as the Nuremberg artisan's house (see pages 28–9) – a square block in the corner of the room where a fire is built under a hooded chimney. Pans would be put either on the coals or on brick plinths above them, while others hung from a jack which regularly twisted over the heat. A bellows stands nearby to help this rather *ad hoc* form of cooking.

The two rooms above are bed-sitting rooms where even the grandest people would meet their guests. This house has an arrangement which reappeared in the 19th century. A hidden tank in a tall cupboard drops water into a pewter washbasin below, very useful for washing hands after eating (forks for eating were not yet used in Northern Europe after their invention in Italy in the 16th century).

Another kitchen in a German house, hung as usual with huge pieces of pewter, has other, more recognizable items. A mezzaluna, still used for cutting herbs, hangs beside the cooking fire, as does a pierced colander and funnel; there are rough pottery jugs similar to those that you can buy in Mediterranean markets today, a garishly painted cupboard and a string bag, like those still made in France, hangs on the back of the door ready for shopping. It is somehow reassuring to know that although Europe was riven by wars and religious turmoil, although books were the preserve of the richest and cleverest people, and although countries were just emerging from the Dark Ages, cooks went shopping with string bags like we do and little girls showed their dolls how to chop herbs.

Looking at these densely furnished little houses, it would seem that the owners just could not stop buying miniature objects. Can kitchens really have been so over-stocked that the cook risked being brained by falling colanders? Consider the 17th century Dutch kitchen room, a one-off for a would-be

◁ This walnut cabinet house comes from Basel in Switzerland and was owned by the Wengen family in around 1700. A dish, marked by the Basel goldsmith Peter Biermann, dates from 1709. Although of only three rooms, the house is large and beautifully detailed.

△ Sometimes the dolls had to be content with one room – but this
Dutch cabinet kitchen from the 17th century is packed with interest. The
floor and walls are hand-painted, as is the realistic fire behind the kettles.
There are egg baskets, beer barrels, egg poachers and an axe all to hand.

cook to play with, which comes in its own charming arched cabinet. Every corner of space is filled with racks, plates, moulds and provisions, and even the walls and floor are jollied up with paint.

The Swiss kitchen on the opposite page, part of a walnut cabinet house originally owned by the Wengen family of Basel in 1700, is a great deal tidier. The characteristic stove has an arched base for storing the carefully cut logs for fuel, and above this is a two-tier cooking area. A copper kettle sits at the top, keeping warm all day, while on the larger hob is an assortment of copper pans and lidded jugs. The whole stove and the walls are a brilliant emerald green and, presumably, tiled.

This relatively simple house has a large storage area in the basement where a set of curious, red-painted palings seem to

guard a row of wine and beer barrels – perhaps a horse was stabled here as in the Kress house on pages 24–5.

Another green-tiled stove can be spotted in the top room which has a set of large chargers balanced above the panelling – a common feature in houses of this date. But some of these chargers are silver rather than pewter and one by the Basel goldsmith Peter Biermann is dated 1709. Behind the chargers, a fine swirling pattern of foliage and flowers has been painted, while on the panelling hangs a lantern clock with its long, hanging pendulum and weights – the precursor of the more common longcase clock.

While most of the furnishings in the middle room of this three-roomed house were added during the 19th century, the storage area and the upper room are original.

A NUREMBURG HOUSE

It is easy to imagine the German city of Nuremberg as it was in the 17th century because it was one of the favoured visits of the 18th-century grand tourists and, as such, much illustrated. Nuremberg was also a city of great importance up to the 17th century, having a fine castle which was a favourite residence of the German emperors. It was surrounded by a large moat and, inside that, a city wall and, partly as a defence and partly for show, there were no fewer than 365 towers in the city. The artist, Albrecht Dürer, was born in Nuremberg, and it remained an independent city until 1806 when it was annexed to Bavaria.

An engraving of 1658 shows its fine central square: the ground floors of the houses have arched doors and shaded stalls for shops; three or four storeys up, the roofs culminate in turrets and dormer windows. The engraving celebrates a strange event – the parade of a giant sausage – but shows all the burghers on parade, with their wives looking on from upstairs windows. There are dogs, peddlars and the town band, too.

The dolls' house owned by the Bethnal Green Museum of Childhood in London could be a carbon copy of a house in the square, except that the builder has not attempted more than three storeys. It is dated 1673 – 15 years after the engraving – but nothing has changed. Here is the pleasant soft arch of the doorway, with carefully cut stone and the tiny panes of glass (blowers were not able to make them bigger at this period) can also be spotted in the engraving. Most significant of all is the central window on the roof with its metal star; real houses in the city were decorated with all kinds of finials and flags until the metal ones were banned because they kept falling and injuring passers-by.

Although this Nuremberg house is not the earliest or grandest, it is the first artisan's house to exist and was probably made as a toy, because its scale suits the height of a young girl.

△ The arched door and small-paned windows of this real, surviving Nuremberg house are virtually identical to those of the dolls' house. The spikes on the roofs of real houses were removed because they were so dangerous when they fell.

DATE Made in 1673

SCALE 108cm (42½in) high, 92cm (36in) wide, 47cm (18½in) deep.

STRUCTURE The dolls' house is made from pine and painted to look like stone with a roof painted to resemble tiles. The heavy front door – security was important at this period – has a solid looking metal handle and lock with, inside, a hanging bell. The facade splits into two almost equal doors which open below the central dormer window with its metal star.

LAYOUT OF ROOMS A simple box with only four rooms. Downstairs there is a dining room with pewter-filled walls (and a boxed-off privy), while the other ground-floor room is a kitchen filled with casks, utensils and plates, with a charcoal cooking stove at the back. Upstairs there are two bedrooms, each with a ceramic stove – the right-hand room seems to double up as a sitting room.

KEY AND SCALE

1	2
3	4

1 Bedroom
2 Bedroom
3 Dining room
4 Kitchen

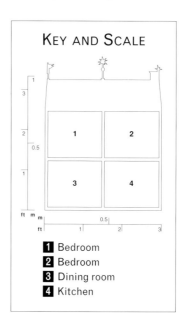

▷ This little doll dressed all in black seems to be a good luck chimney sweep. The superstition that chimney sweeps bring good luck – especially if you bow and say good morning to them – is still observed in some parts of Northern Europe and Britain.

◁ Tiny but perfect, this little needlework box is a miniature version of the kind of luxury object a Nuremberg lady would have kept for her sewing.

△ This simple, four-roomed dolls' house would have originally belonged to an artisan rather than a rich merchant and is one of the first of its kind.

◁ Bedrooms in German houses still have solid painted cupboards such as this and they will still be filled with quantities of padded bedding in cheerful fabrics. There will be quilts, duvets and pillows and other linen items.

▷ Hens would be kept indoors in the winter as a ready source of fresh meat and, with luck, fresh eggs. These hens are actually covered with tiny feathers.

▷ The chair with its pierced back splat is a typically Bavarian design that can still be found in kitchens and inns today. The heart-shaped cut out is both decorative and useful when carrying the chair. The high-backed chair with decorated stretchers (also a typical Bavarian design) was popular all over Europe in the 17th century. This one is upholstered in floral fabric.

▷ Like all early dolls' houses, this one has a fully stocked kitchen, showing us exactly how they cooked on hot coals in the 17th century. The circular hanging rack would be placed above the fire while the flat metal grill would sit directly on the heat. The fish rack, complete with fish, is a toy which comes down from Roman times.

The Nuremberg house on the previous page may be the earliest toy dolls' house to exist but there is another surviving Nuremberg house of note — the Baumler house. A typically overstocked German house of the late 17th century, it also holds an extremely rare set of poured-wax dolls made with solid bases so that they can stand up without support. One upper room in the house holds no less than four dolls of various ages in elaborate, wide, spangled dresses. Two stand alone beside a large central table surrounded by heavy velvet upholstered chairs. There are oval portraits on the walls, bunches of mixed flowers in ornate silver vases, more silver for the sconces on the walls, and windows carefully made from the small and thick blown glass of the period. As in so many of these German homes, a large, green ceramic stove heats the room .

The Baumler house is especially interesting because it includes a trading room in a vaulted basement where the merchant-owner would have worked (home offices are nothing new). It is a homely place, much simpler than the reception rooms above. The merchant would have worked at a wooden trestle table, now stocked with a large candle and pair of scissors. One wall is lined with shelves holding goblets, jugs and jars of wood and metal, with square drawers below to hold loose provisions, and other large boxes stacked on shelves. There is a large weighing scale beside them accompanied by a careful set of weights. Another wall holds a closed cupboard and open shelves, decorated with a gable top, which are stacked with different sizes of writing paper. A female doll, with her hair in a typically German neat plait, overlooks the office.

Like other German houses of the period, this one has two fine horses waiting in the stable along with their haybox and grooming brushes, while a charming courtyard holds a later, 18th-century, model of a coach. Behind, an artist has painted a symmetrical garden with flower beds and fountains leading to a pavilion. Though later items have been added here, the atmosphere of 17th-century Southern Germany remains.

OLD AMSTERDAM

Similarly, old Amsterdam of the late 17th century is evoked by the cabinet house assembled by Petronella de la Court, who married a rich Amsterdam brewer called Oortman, whose initials appear on the back of a settle in the cabinet. Nothing has been stinted in this *nouveau riche* house.

Petronella obviously imagined that her doll had just had a baby, for there she is, in the obligatory lying-in room, which is richly decorated with faux wood and chunky balusters. She lounges in a curtained box bed with two other very smart dolls. They sit at two tables absolutely covered with porcelain and sweetmeats over lace-edged table cloths. On the walls are

▽ The imaginary merchant of the late 17th-century German Baumler house worked from home. His blue painted office displays large cheeses, weighing scales and cupboards full of ledgers.

▽ Many early German houses incorporated stables on the ground floor where chunky, spirited horse dolls are kept. The Baumler house has feed baskets, dung shovels and hay racks.

▷ Cabinets were smart pieces of furniture in the late 17th century and were used for storing valuables, curiosities or, as here, converted into dolls' houses. This example was assembled by Petronella de la Court and inside there is a miniature cabinet of curiosities. It is in the art room where visitors would be expected to admire the owner's collection.

typical garnitures of blue-and-white porcelain. The lying-in room is at the bottom centre of the house, next to a pretty garden of statues on plinths, trelliswork obelisks and a gazebo.

At the other side of the lying-in room is a very smart kitchen, more for show than for use. Above the garden is another typical feature of rich 17th-century Dutch life – an art room and cabinet of curiosities. Large oil paintings hang on the wall – one by the Dutch artist Gerard Hoet dated 1674 – and classical busts adorn the shelves. The cabinet, which was so important a feature at a time when continents were being opened up, is filled with tiny "Roman" coins, ivory cutlery, prints and silver.

Between the art room and the music room, which has walls painted with landscapes and gentlemen in full-bottomed wigs ready to play, is a curious two-tier arrangement. In the lower half a nurse walks an older child on leading strings, while in the room above, the man of the house sits at his desk with files and matters of business stacked all around him. On the third of the three floors a maid is busy with the laundry with drying racks stacked over her head while another maid is given a minimal bedroom where she guards the food, peat and firewood – her room is hidden behind palings. This floor also has two fine bedrooms; in one there is a magnificent doll wearing a gauzy headdress and gown trimmed with layers of braid.

PETRONELLA OORTMAN

Petronella Oortman's dolls' house has a rare distinction: it is the subject of a detailed oil painting by the Dutch artist, Jacob Appel (1680–1751). The house dates from between 1686 and 1690, and his painting shows the rooms peopled with dolls in the fashionable clothes of the period.

The elegant dolls, who appear in the painting in conversation, doing the ironing, talking to children in the nursery and taking them about on leading strings, have long since vanished, but the painting also shows that the house not only had glass-fronted doors (still in existence) but that it was covered by filmy curtains, with a pelmet, drawn to keep the sun from fading the contents.

Petronella's house is a high point for the art: the carcase is an immensely detailed and expensive amalgam of tortoiseshell and pewter veneered onto oak, and the panes of glass used for the doors are large and costly for the time. The fittings, too, are made by master craftsmen who have not been asked to economize in any detail – there is, in fact, a legend that it was made to commission for Peter the Great of Russia who reneged on the deal because the end result was too expensive (see page 11). Petronella seems to have had no qualms about the price (reputed to have been 20,000 to 30,000 guilders). She was a wealthy widow when she married the rich silk merchant Johannes Brandt in 1686. Their cipher appears on the sides of the cabinet and throughout the interior.

The furnishings took another 15 years to commission and collect and were fully catalogued in the middle of the 18th century. We therefore know that little was added after that – even though a garden has gone missing.

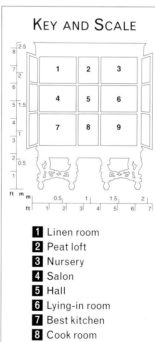

KEY AND SCALE

1	2	3
4	5	6
7	8	9

1 Linen room
2 Peat loft
3 Nursery
4 Salon
5 Hall
6 Lying-in room
7 Best kitchen
8 Cook room
9 Tapestry room

DATE Made between 1686 and 1690, with furnishings up to 1705.
SCALE 255cm (100in) high, 190cm (75in) wide and 78cm (31in) deep.
STRUCTURE Highly ornamented cabinet of veneered tortoiseshell and engraved pewter on oak with two glazed doors. The cabinet sits on a matching stand of two sets of four cabriole legs. These materials are rare in Holland. It seems the maker worked for the French court before coming to Amsterdam.
LAYOUT OF HOUSE The top floor consists of a linen room, a peat loft and a nursery. The middle floor has a central hall with access from the back. At one side of this is a grand salon with the luxurious lying-in room on the other side. On the bottom floor is a central cook room with a dining room (known as the best kitchen) to one side and the tapestry room to the other.

◁ Pieter Janssens' painting shows a calm, light-filled Dutch interior, along with the patterned floor and simple yet sumptuous mix of red chairs and black-framed paintings that can also be seen in the cabinet house.

◁ By the time the Oortman house was created, the mistress had awarded herself a "best kitchen" (bottom left) to show off her dowry and later wealth. The room next door is a servery, below this, hidden in the base, is a cellar.

▽ Rich display began with the entrance hall, always a place to impress guests. The ceiling painting, an allegory of Dawn with attendant putti, is attributed to the real artist, Johannes Voorhout, who supplied other paintings for the lying-in and tapestry rooms.

◁ Behind the tapestry room is a library with a reading desk and chairs. The books include atlases of Africa and East Europe in tooled leather and parchment with marbled end papers. Other books display coats of arms, portraits and townscapes.

▽ In the linen room are two box beds for the maids. These are concealed in the wall and entered through two symmetrical door openings. Above each is an *oeil-de-boeuf* window for ventilation. These are neatly curtained with a tiny floral chintz. Each area has a chair and chamber pot.

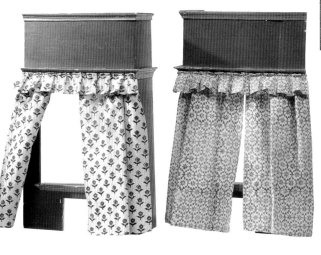

△ The nursery is immensely grand with lacquered exotic birds on the wall and tiny sets of children's clothes. These consist of a nightshirt and pair of loose breeches plus coarse and fine stockings in wool and silk. Other clothes have been lost.

△ No grand 17th- century house was complete without its collectors' cabinet full of curiosities. This one from the tapestry room is filled with exotic shells, piled up in a decorative display, and shows how other cabinets, since emptied, were laid out. The shells were collected and exchanged as marvels of beauty.

Lord Burlington copied ancient
Roman architecture to create
Chiswick House, London,
around 1727, and the triumphal
staircase, balustrades and
three-light Venetian window
appear in the Tate baby house
of c.1760.

CHAPTER TWO

The Age of Grandeur

1700–1780

From Germany and Holland, the
impetus for dolls' house style
moved to England and the houses
that emerged were country houses.
In England itself, the grand
already had palaces and castles
in the country, but now the rich
merchants and the landed squires
began to build Palladian mansions
surrounded by parkland. Unlike the
Dutch and German dolls' houses,
the English houses were not
simple cabinets with interiors.
Their creators made sure that
the dolls' houses were
masterpieces of architectural
detail on the outside too.

The century between 1680 and 1780 is known as the Age of Enlightenment, a period when great thinkers cast away superstition and carefully re-assessed existing ideas and institutions. It was a period of enormous change, unparalleled since the Renaissance in 14th-century Italy. The period produced some of the greatest artists and thinkers in history from Haydn to George Washington, Goethe to Gainsborough, Benjamin Franklin to Mozart, Voltaire to Beethoven. It was, too, a time of great architecture: Les Invalides in Paris and Hampton Court Palace near London were built at the start of the era; followed by the great English country houses – Blenheim, Woburn, Holkham, Harewood and Kedleston – appearing throughout the 18th century. It was, too, the great era of the baby house – a term used for dolls' houses during the 18th century. (Baby being the word for doll at this time.)

△ This miniature Baroque palace comes from Northern Italy and dates from the late 17th century, even if its huge glazed windows, pilasters and entablature are more common to the early 18th century. The windows, which cover almost all the walls, allow the interiors to be clearly seen.

It was far from being a time of peace, however. The nations who generated the great music, painting, architecture and scientific discoveries were constantly at odds.

By 1702, Britain and France were at war, followed by the war of the Austrian Succession, the Jacobite Rising in Scotland, the Seven Years War and the American War of Independence. Yet, somehow through all the turmoil, Europe and America were turning themselves into the civilized nations we still know today; fortunes were being made from agriculture (and spent on the South Sea Bubble or great landed estates) and, when war was temporarily in abeyance, young gentlemen were travelling throughout Europe in search of classical civilizations and romantic landscapes, picking up great works of art along their Grand Tour.

THE NEW FASHIONS

For this reason, although the decorative characteristics of different countries were still sharply idiosyncratic, there was also a great deal of cross-over during this century. At the beginning, the trend was for blue-and-white porcelain, brought from China and Japan along with the much-prized cargos of tea and taken up enthusiastically by the Dutch and, from them, the English. Later, the Scandinavian countries would be inspired by French architecture and applied arts, while the English looked to the works of the 16th-century Italian architect, Andrea Palladio.

By the middle of the 17th century, the great fashions that were to galvanize the 18th century had already begun to appear. Both tea, cocoa and coffee were common drinks by about 1660, tea being known as the China drink and chocolate as the West Indian drink and, with tea from China, came porcelain so fine everyone had to have some. Queen Mary was such an enthusiast that she had Kensington Palace decked out with tiers of blue-and-white and polychrome porcelain from Japan, while German princes had whole rooms dedicated to porcelain – those at Charlottenburg and Oranienburg, for example. And, naturally, dolls' houses had to have their share of blue-and-white.

Mon Plaisir, not so much a dolls' house as an extraordinarily complicated set of rooms created by Princess Augusta Dorothea von Schwarzburg-Arnstadt in the early 18th century, naturally enough had its own porcelain room filled with fine china from Japan, Persia and China, the last with real marks from the Kangxi reign. It also had rococo carved and gilded brackets to support the pieces and mirrored walls. But the Princess went further than creating a series of rooms that included ball rooms, audience chambers and French rooms which mirrored the life at court she would have enjoyed – she began to create an entire town. Her real life was much less fun than her fantasy life. Her husband neglected her, she had no children and she could ill-afford her expensive hobby.

Mon Plaisir itself is much larger in scale than other dolls' houses of this or any other period – the dolls alone are often 31cm (12in) high. They are also copies of real people, including the Princess herself, seen in a fine brocade dress taking tea with a court lady of fashion. All their clothes are immensely complex, following the fashions of 1700 to 1730 as her project progressed. The silk stockings, for instance, are correct in every detail, having been knitted on needles the size of a small pin.

▷ The rooms of Mon Plaisir, created by Princess Augusta Dorothea von Schwarzburg-Arnstadt, portray life in an 18th-century German town. They show the Baroque style at its height. The heavy ceiling mouldings and fire-surrounds, symmetrical arrangements and solid furniture are typical.

▽ Music rooms were a feature of 18th-century grand living. Here a trio and impressive diva are in a room decorated with hunting murals. Judging by their clothes, they are gently-born amateurs. One plays the clavichord, another a flute and the third a type of banjo.

ANN SHARP'S DOLLS' HOUSE

A portrait of Queen Anne hangs over the drawing room fire in Ann Sharp's cupboard house – rightly so for this house was given by the Queen to her god-daughter, one of fourteen children born to John Sharp, Archbishop of York. Another picture is of Bishopthorpe Palace, where the archbishops still live, while a third, in a bedroom, is of Mother Shipton, the Yorkshire seer (and probably witch) who was a well-known figure of the time.

The house can be dated to about 1700. Ann Sharp was born in 1691, Queen Anne died in 1714, and a piece of silver in the house is hallmarked 1686. Although many of the original pieces remain, Ann continued to play with the house until her death around 1771 and bought miniatures for the rooms throughout her life. It therefore mirrors the taste of most of the 18th century.

One charming feature of the house is that Ann named many of the dolls who live there and, with a little piece of paper pinned to their clothes, denoted their station in life. The owner is "My Lord Rochett", whose heir, "William" sits by the witch's picture. There are guests like the indignant "Lady Jemima Johnson" and "Mrs Lemon", and all the servants from "Roger, ye butler" to "Fanny Long, ye chambermaid". Although the house has no facade, the objects inside reveal much of 18th-century life. There are silver candles and snuffers, objects of shell and straw-work fashionable in the 18th century, and bleeding cups for the sick. Even the blankets have "clocks" – little embroideries that identified them – in this case they are little flowers veined in scarlet.

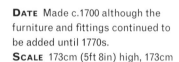

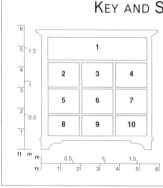

KEY AND SCALE

1	Storage/Attic
2	Bedroom
3	Boudoir
4	Lying-in room
5	Drawing room
6	Dining room
7	Kitchen
8	Servants' room
9	Servants' room
10	Storeroom

DATE Made c.1700 although the furniture and fittings continued to be added until 1770s.

SCALE 173cm (5ft 8in) high, 173cm (5ft 8in) wide, 53cm (1ft 9in) deep.

STRUCTURE Simple cupboard, originally with solid doors and later with glazed doors. The chimney pieces are of picture moulding painted like marble, some in the corners of the room as was fashionable. The doors are papered over to match the walls, another fashionable feature. There is a built-in red lacquer corner cupboard. The whole is quite crude.

LAYOUT OF ROOMS There are nine rooms and, at the top of the house, shelves to display surplus dolls and furniture. The top storey has an important bedroom, a lying-in room and Milady's boudoir; below is a drawing room, dining room/hall and kitchen with spit. At the bottom are the servants' rooms (they moved to the attic in the late 18th century) and what seems to be a storeroom.

△ The interior of a room in Ham House, England (early 17th century). The house was a pioneering example much copied. Not surprisingly similar features turn up later in Ann Sharp's house.

◁ Most grand houses had a lying-in room for new births. The lady of the house might expect a child a year and, if she survived the birth, would spend up to a month here recuperating.

◁ The nine rooms of Ann Sharp's cupboard house reflect early 18th-century life: there is no fixed dining room but a hall set for dining; the servants live in the basement, but their conditions are good. Between the main bedroom and lying-in room, Milady has her own boudoir for privacy.

▷ Ann Sharp continued to buy furniture for her house until her death in 1771. These walnut chairs, some of the crudest seen in these grand houses, probably date from the middle of the 18th century.

▽ The fine detailing in the house includes this brass plate rack stacked with pewter plates. These were common in houses where large dinner parties meant stacks of heavy plates to carry.

▽ Grand 18th-century houses often had built-in theatres for amateur and professional dramatics. Ann Sharp's house has its own miniature toy theatre with a play in progress. There are other toys within the house – including a miniature dolls' house.

◁ Exotic pets were very fashionable in the early 18th century. The lady of the house keeps a parrot in an elegant wire cage. She also has a monkey in her boudoir which wears a shovel-shaped hat.

▷ "My Lord Rochett" wears pink satin trimmed with silver lace, black buckled shoes, silk stockings and a bag wig – such ostentation was fashionable.

△ There was no central heating, no rubber hot-water bottles. Beds were warmed with brass or copper warming-pans filled with red-hot coals. Maids rubbed them over the sheets as the owners and guests prepared for bed.

△ This is one of several English houses known as Edmund Joy's Surprise. They date from the early 18th century, have the curved gables that were so fashionable in Holland, and were often intended as storage for clothes and linen. This one is over 183cm (6ft) high and has hanging space in the centre. The right-hand gable opens to reveal brass-studded doors.

THE ENGLISH BABY HOUSE

The interest in baby houses went right to the top of society. Horace Walpole, writing in 1750, says of Frederick, Prince of Wales, who died the following year, "The Prince is building baby houses at Kew". Frederick had visited the Dowager Duchess of Brunswick some time before and had become fascinated by her project to reproduce the entire court in miniature, hiring local craftsmen to make all the hundreds of objects. At this period, we know of no specific makers of dolls' house furniture and those skilled at actual furniture, silverware, glass blowing and china painting would be hired to create the same objects for dolls.

Certainly no expense was spared either in making or furnishing the houses. Many were created by the estate carpenter – but he was no bodger. The carcase was made with the most exquisite detailing, often in beautiful wood. Quantock, an English baby house made shortly after 1700, is made of oak. Its lower storey is of carved heavy blocks of "ashlar" which lighten on the next floor. Above are beautifully carved columns. Windows are arched, pedimented or rusticated and perfect little finials top the building's balustrade. Inside, fire-

places and doors are carefully detailed and a staircase, which leaves the heaviness of the 17th century behind, stands free in the entrance hall.

One delightful variation on the English dolls' house theme was a cupboard house like the one shown above left made, apparently, by Edmund Joy in the early 18th century. The exteriors of the houses were the Dutch-gabled, many-windowed variety so popular in England at the time, but the interiors, though sometimes covered in wallpaper, were intended for nursery storage with shelves, drawers and cupboards. One of the houses, inscribed, Edmund Joy 1709, was apparently haunted. Another, can be seen at Bethnal Green Museum of Childhood in London.

The Norwich baby house (above), by contrast, is quite small and, although early 18th-century Georgian in style, consists of a single block with heavy quoins and a stalwart front door. It was obviously meant to be a toy and has brass carrying handles at the sides with which the servants could move it around the house. The lock, which is another typically 18th century feature, was there to stop both younger children and curious servants from enjoying the valuable trinkets inside. The

◁ The Norwich baby house is a copy of a typical 18th-century brick-built townhouse with stone decorative quoins and door surround. It is sturdily built, has brass carrying handles at the side and was meant to be used as a toy.

▷ The Yarburgh baby house was made for the family of the same name who lived at Heslington, near York (now the site of York University). It dates from around 1718 and people have speculated that it was designed by the architect of Castle Howard, John Vanbrugh, who married a Yarburgh girl. But, although charming, the design shows no special flair.

fittings, however, have been changed with the years and vary from original features like the kitchen jack and built-in dresser to 19th- century transfer-printed china and printed fabrics.

The Yarburgh baby house, made for the family which until recently lived at Heslington Hall, near York, dates from around 1718 and, like the Norwich house, has the heavy glazing bars of the period. What is, however, unusual, is the way each room is opened via a neat cupboard door with a little ring handle. It is typical of houses, made by the estate carpenter to withstand brutal treatment. One of the Yarburgh girls later married Sir John Vanbrugh, giving rise to a fable that the great architect designed this house. He would probably have been very miffed at the whole idea.

The rooms inside are unexceptional, although most have heavy bolection-mould fireplaces. Upstairs, where the first floor rooms are lower in height than below (a feature soon to be reversed), there are ornate mirrors and fancy wallpaper added later. The top floor rooms, lower still, are intended as bedrooms, for the fireplaces are too good for servants' quarters. As is often the case, the kitchen has suffered least because the details were fitted. The huge dresser, ideal for the large pewter of the period, is genuine, as is the enormous arched alcove for the cooker.

ARCHITECTURAL DETAILS

Baby houses followed the architectural style of real houses. The Tate baby house (see pages 34–5), in the Bethnal Green Museum of Childhood, London, has a very grand staircase and entrance; the stairs sweep up and out in three double flights not unlike the Spanish Steps in Rome and, above the front door, is a Venetian window with a balustrade under and pediment over. Decorative planters sit in front of the balustrade. Once again, the whole is Palladian, with understated windows beside the stairs and two *oeil de boeuf* windows alongside the arched under-door. The ground floor is heavily grand and the *piano nobile* has similar sized windows with pediments. This baby house dates from around 1760 and is over 152cm (5ft) tall. Unlike Quantock, the Tate house is of wood made to simulate stone on the lower floor, window surrounds and quoins with brick on the two upper floors. These sash windows will open and there is even a skylight in the roof. This is seen time and again in real Georgian houses.

Uppark

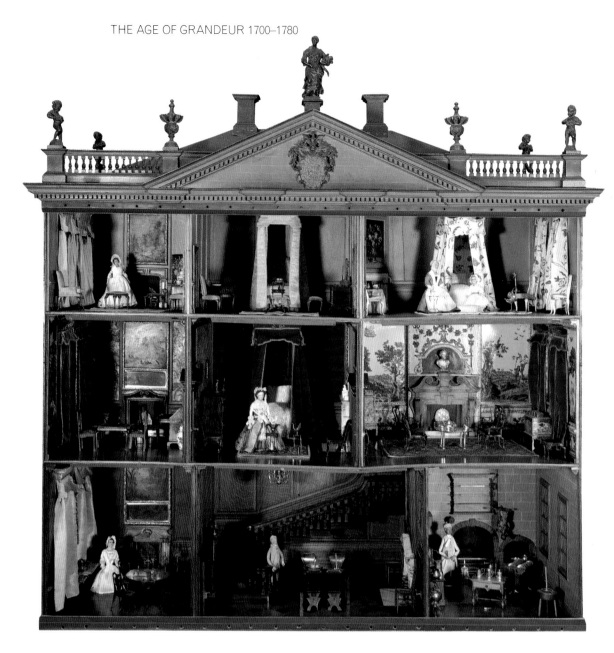

▷ The Nostell Priory baby house was commissioned by Sir Rowland Winn in 1735. To some extent it copies the real Nostell Priory and it is thought that James Paine played a part in its design. Lady Winn and her sister spent long days decorating the rooms with *découpage* scenes and Chinese wallpaper. It is a true example of aristocratic taste of the period.

GRANDIOSE BAROQUE

The baby house at Nostell Priory, Yorkshire, is particularly distinguished because it is believed that the distinguished architect James Paine redesigned part of the house and that Thomas Chippendale created much of its furniture. There is a long-held tradition in the Winn family of Nostell that this is the case. The house is certainly beautiful and dates from around 1735. It is of the most grandiose baroque style with urns and statues above the roof balustrade, a heavy pediment ornamented with the family coat of arms (like Uppark's baby house, see pages 42–7) and large blocks of "stone" carved in the oak basement floor. The staircase is transitional from the heavy 17th-century style to the airy Georgian design and the hall and adjacent drawing room are heavily panelled in oak.

The detail is extraordinary. The floor of the entrance hall is made of light and dark pieces of wood in a pattern of large octagonal and small square tiles (seen in marble in many 18th-century houses), while above the striking pedimented fireplace, a portrait of a black and white dog is inset into the panelling. The drawing room, one of the most complex and beautiful in any dolls' house anywhere, has pedimented mahogany doors, which are carefully gilded, and a swan-neck marble chimneypiece. The wallpaper imitates the fashionable Chinese papers that were imported from the East along with porcelain and tea.

The bedrooms are charming. In one a four-poster is hung with a white ground chintz decorated with informal flowers, while a formal flower painting, after the Dutch, is panelled into the blue painted corner cupboard above the corner-set little fireplace. The bed has its own hand-worked white quilt and the early Georgian chairs are finely carved of ivory. The oak chairs in the panelled ground-floor room are definitely a variation of the style Chippendale was to make his own, as are those in the drawing room above. And, once again, there is the essential little table set with tea-things – but these are grandly made in silver. A visitor to Nostell Priory or Harewood House nearby could walk through rooms that are little different from those in this miniature country palace.

The kitchen, painted in faux buff stonework, has a rack for cooking spits above the fireplace that is found in many baby houses of the period. The kitchen is furnished with some magnificent pieces of contemporary silver – bellied saucepans with turned wooden handles, sugar casters, flour dredgers, mugs, tankards and ornate tea caddies. There is a giant silver kettle which is heated by a flame in a holder underneath (it would have melted if put on the kitchen fire). A wooden plate rack holds a set of silver plates at a convenient waist height. On the other hand, the magnificence is reduced by the presence of a long-tailed ivory mouse.

Not as grandiose as Nostell Priory but almost as fine as the Tate baby house (see page 35) is the architectural detail of the Blackett baby house in the Museum of London. Dating from the mid-18th century, it has a fine double exterior staircase reaching up to the front door with its elegant fanlight while the ground floor is rusticated. The windows carefully follow the precepts of Palladio – ground floor grand but medium size, *piano nobile* large, gracious and airy, top floor small and square. The house has sash windows, seemingly an English invention from the start of the 18th century since Mompesson House, a real house in Salisbury of 1701, has them too.

However, not all 18th-century baby houses were grand affairs. The Westbrook house, made for a middle class child in the early 18th century, is a comparatively small town house that is modestly furnished. Even so, the dining room holds a typical 18th century knifebox with a complete set of pistol-grip knives made of brass; the spit in the kitchen has its own roasting goose and there is a silver footwarmer.

Unlike many dolls' houses of the period, this one seems to be almost authentic (although some of the wooden dolls in contemporary clothing have replacement wooden heads). The Westbrook house gives, in immense detail, a true picture of everyday life in the early 18th century. Each piece was made for little Miss Westbrook, who lived on the Isle of Dogs on the outskirts of London, by local tradesmen as a thank-you to her father, a property owner who was moving house.

AMERICA JOINS IN

The earliest surviving American dolls' house is confusingly dated both 1744 and 1774, one date on each side of the upper floor, but it seems that it was made around the earlier date, the second being added to celebrate, perhaps, a change of ownership. Known as the Van Cortlandt Mansion, it was actually made for the Homans family of Boston, descending to the Greenoughs of Long Island who gave it to the Van Cortlandts. It is clearly an American colonial house with little to connect it to English baby houses. In fact, it is much more closely Dutch or German in style, with a fancy gable and mansard roof. It stands on a large drawer, intended for dolls' furniture storage, and two rooms on two storeys open on both front and back of the building. Like 19th-century mass-produced dolls' houses, this American version has solved the problem of two girls wanting to play at the same time. It has brass carrying handles on either side, a shutter opening into the loft and two decorated columns hold up the open sections of the building. Sash windows are painted on the blank sides. It is one of the earliest surviving dolls' houses that was a true toy.

△▷ The interior of the Blackett baby house, made between 1740–1745, is true to the period. The over-scaled, colourful walls are hand-painted – though, in reality, they would be papered. The gilded frames, architectural features and mirrors are intended to catch the candlelight and add glitter. It can be seen at the Museum of London.

KING STREET BABY HOUSE

A chance view of an 18th-century baby house found in Torquay in 1984 led a dolls' house enthusiast to realize that its strictly classical facade

△ This is the real 27 King Street in the centre of King's Lynn in Norfolk. Ironically its balustraded top was only added after the discovery of the King Street baby house. Being an exact copy of the original building, it provided conservationists with the pattern.

was identical to that of 27 King Street in the Norfolk town of King's Lynn. This makes the baby house a very rare one indeed for, unlike the grand houses of Uppark and Nostell Priory, most dolls' houses of this type cannot be identified as being based on actual buildings. Although the baby house is missing the real building's fan light, in virtually all other respects it is identical. However, until recently there was one major difference, the real building was missing the balustrade at the top of the house (as a result of a 19th-century gale). This has now been put back (see above), based on evidence from the baby house.

Further detective work found that, although this is an English baby house, it was probably made for the daughter of a Rotterdam merchant, Hubert Vlierden or Flierden, who lived in the house and married from there in 1715. He is known to have had a daughter, Ann, so it was more than likely made for her. The size and scale of the house is also reminiscent of earlier German houses.

Unfortunately, when it was discovered the baby house was empty of all its contents. It is now filled with painstakingly collected or re-created furniture and dolls representing life in the mid-18th century. Because Vlierden was a banker working from the house and because 27 King Street remained a bank until 1861, a counting house was made in the baby house using archive material from the real bank of Coutts.

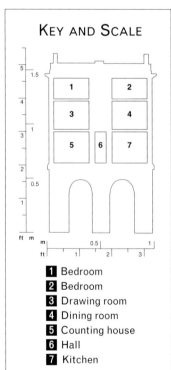

KEY AND SCALE

1 Bedroom
2 Bedroom
3 Drawing room
4 Dining room
5 Counting house
6 Hall
7 Kitchen

DATE Made c.1740, although the furniture has come from diverse sources and some has been specially made.

SCALE 104cm (3ft 5in) high, 105cm (3ft 7in) wide, 54cm (21in) deep.

STRUCTURE Made of wood, it stands on a high rusticated, arched base to bring it to playing level. Hinged panels open on either side of the front door. There are three floors with the top floor having lower ceilings. The front door opens separately to reveal stairs. This layout bears no resemblance to the real King's Lynn building.

LAYOUT OF ROOMS The integral bank or counting house (a common feature in houses of the 18th century) and the kitchen are on the ground floor; above it are the first floor drawing room and dining room with, on top, an adult and child's bedroom.

◁ Although the house lacked all its furniture when it was discovered on the south coast, the building is notable for its integral architectural features. The main rooms are panelled and careful scraping has revealed their original colours – dull green, yellows, browns and black.

▽ The pediment over the door and the simple panelling would have been highly fashionable in a provincial town like King's Lynn.

◁ Architectural details include the heavy chimney pieces with overmantels that are typical of the early 18th century. The overmantel would have held a mirror or oil painting, while the jutting centre of the mantelpiece was designed for a clock or ornament. The grate is also typical of the period.

▷ Although the furniture in the kitchen are replacements, the four spit holders above the grate are original. The 20th-century reconstruction aims to reproduce life in mid-18th century King's Lynn, Norfolk.

ELABORATE CABINETS

While in England during the 18th century baby houses were in vogue, in Holland and in Sweden smart cabinet houses remained popular. Sara Ploos van Amstel's magnificent Dutch cabinet house (above) was assembled in the 18th century from three different late 17th-century houses. It has exactly the same kind of porcelain room that could be found at Charlottenburg, Oranienburg and Kensington Palace, showing how quickly dolls' houses caught up with fashions in real decorating. The "porcelain" (actually painted glass because Europe had not yet discovered the secret of making high-fired porcelain) is displayed on little brackets which reach right up

the walls and which hold the larger, grander pieces while a display cabinet is stuffed full of guglets and juglets, vases and bottles in true Chinese style. In front is a tiny table surrounded by hard-back chairs that are typical of late 17th-century style both in Holland and Britain. The table is laid with more porcelain for taking tea. The little cups, like their real Chinese counterparts, are without handles.

Similar chairs and porcelain carefully displayed, appear in the Swedish dolls' house of c.1746 shown opposite. The chairs are of heavy card and gilded. They have cabriole legs and heavy splat backs and, as was the fashion in the 18th century, are lined up against the wall. There were no set dining rooms at the time and the fashion was to open up a folding table and arrange the chairs for an impromptu party. Behind each chair is a mirrored sconce with large candlestick. This, of course, was in fashion throughout 18th-century Europe, but Sweden then, as now, was preoccupied with lighting, and the mirrors are larger and the sconces more numerous than you would find in southern Europe. The dolls' house porcelain was actually made in Stockholm in 1746. This is extremely early – England had only learnt how to make porcelain in 1745. Charmingly, too, this little Swedish house has its own tiled stove. A similar Norwegian house (c.1730) has imitation Dutch tiles cladding the open hearth in the kitchen, the area where both family and servants ate together. In the drawing room, decorated with the most eccentric "Chinese" wallpaper of exploding trees and enormous birds, the table is, once more, laid for tea, complete with porcelain pot and handleless cups.

A Dutch house, built around 1748 and known as the Gontard house, is particularly well stocked with food of the period. There are sacks of peas, beans, rice, barley, millet and lentils – dried food for use in the winter. Butter is kept in barrels and twisted into rolls for the table. Preserved meat hangs from the walls – hams, smoked meat and North

European sausages – and there are jars of sweet and savoury preserves, jams and pickles, dried fruit and mushrooms emphasizing that the only way of keeping foods was the traditional methods of preserving in sugar, vinegar or smoke. There's a basket of poultry, including Bohemian pheasants and woodcock. This 18th-century larder also has bottles of oil and vinegar, mustard, truffles, sugar loaves in quantity and coffee.

TOYS FOR WHOM

As we have seen in chapter one, many of these superb cabinet houses were not, of course, made as toys. They were the playthings of grown women living in great houses who could indulge their decorative fantasies in miniature. Perhaps this was a way to ease the frustrations of not being able to decorate real houses, which in England were generally designed, coloured, furnished and carpeted by such designers as Adam and Wyatt. Children, however, were not totally excluded from this miniature world as they were in Holland. Flora Gill Jacobs explains that some dolls' houses were even made for children "… even though in most cases the children were permitted only to look at them – and on state occasions at that. Almost all of them are occupied by large families of dolls."

◁ When closed, Sara Ploos van Amstel's house resembles a sturdy walnut bureau with a garniture of blue-and-white porcelain on the top (very fashionable in the 18th century). The cabinet house has its own room filled with tiny copies of Chinese and Japanese blue-and-white, displayed in specially fitted cupboards and wall brackets.

▷ This Swedish house, c.1746, comes in a charming, glazed cupboard with characteristic cabriole legs and arched top. You can see the immaculate rooms through the glass doors.

▷ The room below the arch is symmetrically laid out and has a ceramic tiled stove to the left. Below are cabriole legged chairs, formally aligned, each with a mirror behind to catch the precious northern light. The formality and elegance, along with the shining black and white floor, show the French influence in 18th-century Scandinavia.

The grand 18th-century terraces of the fashionable spa town of Bath have inspired this simple late 18th-century small dolls' house. The heavy ashlar treatment of the ground floor terrace and its windows, along with the emphasis placed on the front door and window above it, are common to both.

CHAPTER THREE

The Classical Age

1780–1840

As wealth began to trickle down from the powerful aristocrats and wealthy merchants to the middle classes, so middle-class buildings in squares, terraces and crescents grew up in major towns. Smaller towns saw grand, detached town houses arrive on main streets for the local bigwigs. Pleased with their new status, the well-to-do made dolls' houses to the same standard for their daughters and, through them, we can picture the daily life of the urban middle classes.

History is not littered with periods when it was fun to be a child. But if one were to pick a time when well-to-do children were given both freedom and attention, the late Georgian and Regency period would be a good choice. You need only look at pictures of children at the end of the 18th century to see that they are enjoying themselves. They are wearing attractive and, more important, comfortable clothes, even in formal portraits. They have toys – pull-along horses, hoops and tops; they have numerous pets, from dogs to baby deer – and they are nearly all smiling.

In 1785, John Singleton Copley painted the three youngest daughters of George III having lots of fun. Princess Mary is waving her tambourine and pulling Princess Amelia along in her very smart baby carriage; Princess Sophia holds her hand; three spaniels cavort in the front, and parrots pick grapes above the pretty scene. In a charming painting of 1803 by William Beechey of the Croft children, five-year-old Thomas is making bubbles from a clay pipe, while Mary Ellen Best, in 1833, shows a York couple in their garden, with two of their children climbing about on the gate posts.

As the 18th century progressed, advanced thinkers moved from solving the abstract problems of politics and the State and of social customs and science to putting their ideas into action. In the 19th century, steam engines turned into trains, new cooking ranges appeared and various forms of agricultural machines were created. Slavery was abolished, and the idea of universal education gradually emerged.

THE NEW TEACHING

Children's education during the end of the 18th and start of the 19th century was heavily influenced by Maria Edgeworth, a novelist who had brought up her own brother and had therefore turned her thoughts to training the young. Although she was well aware of the importance of toys in education, following the lead of the French philosopher, Rousseau, who suggested that dolls would encourage little girls in dress sense, she was puritanical about which toys were educational and which were not. Dolls and dolls'

houses tended to be put in the latter group. They were educational all right – but they taught the wrong things.

Maria Edgeworth explained her reservations: "our objections to dolls are offered with great submission and due hesitation. With more confidence we may venture to attack Baby Houses; an unfinished Baby House might be a good toy, as it would employ little carpenters and seamstresses to fit it up; but a completely furnished Baby House proves as tiresome to a child as a furnished seat is to a young nobleman. After peeping, for in general only a peep may be had into each apartment, after being thoroughly satisfied that nothing is wanting, and that consequently there is nothing to be done, the young lady lies her doll upon the state bed… and falls fast asleep in the midst of her felicity."

Did Maria Edgeworth ever watch a little girl playing with a dolls' house? The quotation above makes it hard to believe that she did, even though she is right that uncompleted toys are greater fun. But when is a dolls' house ever complete?

For all this, Maria Edgeworth makes it clear that education should begin early and that it should be fun – two ideas that we firmly go along with today. She also emphasizes that children should not be punished for breaking their toys – curiosity which might lead to harm should still be encouraged.

There had certainly been a change of attitude towards children, no longer were they kept out of the way. Parents were more concerned about their upbringing and education than they had been in the past. It was recognized that children could learn from educational toys and these included dolls' houses.

By the mid-18th century, the Palladian style so suited to the period had gained the upper hand in both real and dolls' houses. Its perfect proportions, immaculate detailing and love of classical ornament (shown right, rather heavy-handedly, in an "ashlar" baby house of around 1760 which seems almost made of building block) went hand in hand with the need to combine nature with building, with a love of light indoor spaces and a need for order.

◁ This smart English lady doll (c.1780) wears the *décolleté*, flat-fronted bodice and wide, although unflounced, skirt of the reign of Queen Anne.

▷ The architecture of this simple carpenter-made house is extremely grand. Heavy blocks of ashlar, the three-light windows and the formal doorway are emphasized by columns and a pediment. Although early 18th century in style, it dates from the middle of the century.

AUDLEY END

This may look like a simple dolls' house but Audley End is one of the most interesting of the period. It was almost certainly made for the eight children of Richard, third Lord Braybrooke and his wife, Lady Jane Cornwallis, daughter of the Marquess of Cornwallis, some time after 1825. A painting of the Audley End nursery (c.1850), shows it clearly.

The dolls' house has never been removed from the real house (in Essex), now run by English Heritage, and its interior design mirrors the interior of Audley End itself, which Lord Braybrooke redesigned in the 1820s. Indeed, scraps of fabric used in the house turn up again in the dolls' house and have, in turn, been used to re-create Audley End's Regency decor.

It tells us much about early 19th-century life – the lively colours, the gaming tables and musical instruments – when children were encouraged to enjoy themselves. The house also contains hand-decorated chinoiserie pieces of furniture. These were made by J. Bubb, an important London maker, who has never been known to decorate furniture. The probability is that Louisa, Marchioness Cornwallis, a talented artist (her chinoiserie firescreens still exist at Audley End) and the children's grandmother, embellished them for her grandchildren.

△ The Ivies, Church Street, Ashbourne, Derbyshire ,was built around 1785. It and the Audley End dolls' house, created about 30 years later, share the Palladian order of windows and the roofs of both are hidden by a pediment.

▷ The dolls' house seen from the open back gives a startling glimpse of the brilliant colours and liveliness of Regency style. Audley End itself would have looked similar after redecoration in 1825.

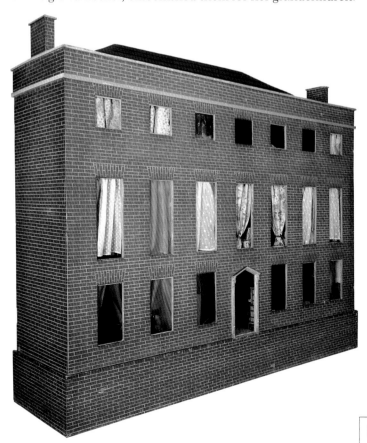

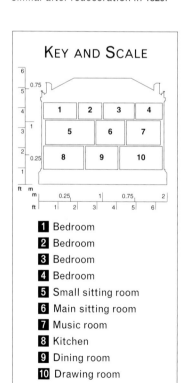

KEY AND SCALE

1	2	3	4
5	6	7	
8	9	10	

1 Bedroom
2 Bedroom
3 Bedroom
4 Bedroom
5 Small sitting room
6 Main sitting room
7 Music room
8 Kitchen
9 Dining room
10 Drawing room

DATE Later than 1825. The Braybrooke's first child was born in 1820; the watercolour of the dolls' house *in situ* dates from the 1850s.

SCALE 165cm (5ft 5in) high, 193cm (6ft 6in) wide.

STRUCTURE Carpenter-made of painted wood. The house is a simple box with entry through the open back (which may have been glazed). In appearance it is like an extended town house, with characteristic large first-floor windows and servants' rooms above. Architectural detail is minimal.

LAYOUT OF ROOMS Four bedrooms on the top floor (no bathrooms nor stairs). The first, and main, floor has a sumptuous music room, furnished landing and small sitting room. The ground floor has a large kitchen, elegant dining room and a drawing room rather less grand than the music room.

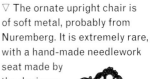

▽ The ornate upright chair is of soft metal, probably from Nuremberg. It is extremely rare, with a hand-made needlework seat made by the designer.

▽ Bone and antler furniture became popular at the turn of the 18th century. Dolls' houses followed the trend as this bone table shows.

◁ This glazed chest on chest (and pair of pier tables in the music room) were made by J. Bubb but, because no painted piece from the firm is known, the chance is that the chinoiserie was painted by the children's grand-mother, a noted artist.

▷ Porcelain plates hand-painted in high Regency fashion with Greek key borders, classical motifs and brilliant flowers. Iron red and gilding are typical of the period.

△ Over-scale clock by Evans & Cartwright, tin toymakers of Wolverhampton. Probably designed for a bracket, it is painted "foxy red" to imitate mahogany.

▷ Daybed of cardboard, probably home-made, is covered in a pretty glazed chintz with a pattern of pinks. The fabric is also used for the sitting room curtains.

▷ A very rare piece: this unusual blue wash-stand with its original ewer and basin was made by the English toymaker Evans & Cartwright with gaily painted flower decoration.

◁ The Princesses' house, dating from around 1801, seems to have been made by a ship's carpenter for the daughters of George III. This is probable, because it is fairly crude. The house was a holiday project for the girls to paint and decorate.

▷ The bedroom of the Princesses' house has a cosy bed with wool hangings and simple furniture including a rush-seated chair and washstand. The original bell pull hangs beside the bed and still rings a bell in the hall.

MAKE DO AND MEND

Many parents followed the idea that toys were educational. One old lady writing in the 1870s about the dolls stored in her nursery chest, recalls: "When I had plenty of time to spare, I used to arrange them in smaller drawers of another chest, four storeys high, which made a capital dolls' house, quite as neat and commodious as any of the 'family mansions, replete with every requisite convenience' which one sees advertised so abundantly in the morning papers.

"I never had a proper dolls' house bought for me. Mama always liked me to invent my own playthings, and then she said they both lasted longer and I enjoyed them more. I believe she was quite right, for I had the fun of inventing…. I don't think the girls of today, with their miniature dinner parties and their real mould of blancmange and soups and open tarts which have been made specially for them in the kitchen by a proper cook, have any idea how Lucy and I enjoyed keeping house

upon two lumps of sugar and a piece of seedcake in that dear old oriel window, with pieces of writing-paper turned up at the corners for dishes and nut-shells for cups and saucers.

"I'm sure we got a lot more satisfaction, real, lasting, solid satisfaction, out of our four-storey chest of drawers with papa's old cigar boxes for beds and acorn cups for toilet services and half-a-dozen empty pillboxes for stools and square pieces of wood supported on cotton-reels for tables and little round bits of cardboard for plates and dishes, than children get now from their toyshop dining-rooms and drawing-rooms and bedrooms with real furniture and sets of proper crockery and things that are always getting broken and spoilt."

Of course, this is a lament for the good old days in which the elderly always indulge. But this writer was right in looking back on a good and simple childhood.

If a hand-written note found inside the front door of a simple pine baby house (shown above left and above) of around

six stools to accommodate a party. There is also a tin fireplace painted with roses, a leather-covered work box and a little mahogany Pembroke table. The bedroom is simpler, with a four-poster bed with woolwork hangings, dressing table, rush-seated armchair and original wallpaper. The bell pulls, drawing-room fireplace and architectural features still exist in this charming toy.

We know about Captain Grey, the fourth son of General Sir Charles Grey, later 1st Earl Grey, who was given the command of the Royal Yacht, *Princess Augusta*, in 1801. He and his wife Mary Whitbread had several children.

AMERICAN PURITANS

Britain, during this period, was one of the leaders in liberal education, with even American children being taught from British school primers. But parents in the United States were far less liberal in their attitudes. *A Present to Children*, published in New London in 1783, shows little sign of modern thought: "Improve your time. When you play, do it because God gives you leave. Learn to get good and do good in your plays." Meanwhile, *Song for a Little Miss*, condemned dolls' houses as frivolous, and pleasure in "glittering shelves, tiny tables, plates and chairs of her Baby Room" as a waste of God's time. A song follows: "Fain would I guard this prattling voice/These haughty airs surprise; No more shall baubles be my choice/Nor plays, nor idleness."

This general condemnation of dolls and their houses emerges, predictably enough, at a time when the playthings had at last become commonly available and the toy industry began to gear itself up to create those "glittering shelves, tiny tables, plates and chairs".

1801–1804 is to be believed, the love of simplicity extended to the very top of society. The note read "This Dolls House was made by the Children of George the Third then staying at Weymouth and given by them to the Children of the Honourable Sir George Grey my Grandfather, who was Flag Captain on the Kings Ship. Mary Bonham Carter" (the last being the name of the writer, not the ship). It is more likely, however, that the house was made by a ship's carpenter and given to the King's children as a holiday project for them to paint the furniture – although the embroidery on the bed hangings is almost certainly professional.

The dolls' house has only painted windows and consists of two rooms, a bedroom and a drawing room with a narrow hall and landing. Painted to look like ashlar (in a much simpler way than the house on page 57), it has feet more suited to a country chest of drawers. The two rooms both have gros-point carpets, the drawing room having two sofas, five armchairs and

△ This charming small wax doll (c.1800) is English and wears a child's clothes – not very different from an adult's – dating from the early 19th century. The Biedermeier sofa (c.1820) behind her, with original upholstery, is German and of crude wood painted to simulate rosewood.

THE NEW TOYMAKERS

Dolls and their furnishings were the first things to arrive – commercially-made dolls' houses came later. Perhaps because the simple, flat-fronted terraced middle-class houses of the 1840s were easily made, without patterns, by carpenters and skilled amateurs and the plain carpenter-made house is typical of the early part of Victorian era.

This type of house is exemplified by the two carpenter-made Georgian-style dolls' houses featured right and far right. The three-storey house (right) has obviously been well played with but unfortunately has no furnishings. It has three floors with two rooms on the top floor, one large room in the middle and two rooms on the bottom floor.

The two-storey dolls' house (far right) from the Elizabethan Museum, Great Yarmouth, Norfolk, has also had a great deal of use. This house has four large rooms and is fully furnished inside, although the furnishings are not all original and have been added to as late as the early 20th century.

In the early 19th century English toymakers mostly consisted of small firms and individual London makers like Bubb (see page 59 for an example of his work), who stamped his name on the pieces. The Wolverhampton firm of Evans & Cartwright was founded in 1802 and made tin dolls' house furniture until 1850.

Much of the new toy industry was centred in Germany, reaching Britain through the links between the two royal families. Queen Victoria and her mother both played with the neat, jointed little wooden dolls that were both made at, and named after, the German region of Grödnertal. Victoria played with her large group of dolls until she was at least 12 years old, and she and her governess, Baroness Lehzen, sewed their typical Regency outfits which have high waists, low bodices and tiny puffed sleeves. She is known to have made

▷ The simulated blocks of stone of this early 19th-century dolls' house are huge but the paintwork is original. The front door also opens, although a child would open the house by the catch left of the front door. This carpenter-made house is of simple design.

◁ Although the house no longer has its furniture, the old kitchen range still exists. As the house dates from before 1840, this kind of range can still be found in untouched cottage kitchens. There are shelves for implements rather than a dresser.

△ This carpenter-made dolls' house at the Elizabethan House Museum, Great Yarmouth, Norfolk, has bricks painted on to a wooden base. As with other dolls' houses of the period it is difficult to date exactly but the style is certainly early 19th century. The house opens straight down the front and it has been much used.

costumes for 32 of the dolls and her governess for the remaining 100. Only seven are men, while others with plump faces were chosen to be women they knew and have longer skirts than the fine featured dolls who are dancers.

German imports also reached the United States – not only because their manufacturing skills made them less expensive than home-grown toys but also because their years of experience in producing toys had given them authenticity and charm. In December 1837, the Philadephia Public Ledger announced that Christmas and New Year presents had just arrived from Germany: "fine toys, wax dolls… and furniture and fittings for baby houses".

Dolls' houses, on the other hand, were harder to mass produce and ship, and so local craftsmen or skilled amateurs (as in Britain) made American versions that were then filled with German furniture. An example of an American hand-made dolls' house that contains some rare German Walterhausen furniture is the well-documented Reverend Brett house on the following pages.

63

REVEREND BRETT

We know so much about the Brett house and its owners that it provides us with a charming glimpse of middle-class New York life in the first half of the 19th century. It was built by the Reverend Dr Philip Milledoler Brett, working in the sail loft of the family shipping business in South Street, New York, between 1838 and 1840, when he was in his early twenties.

The building is a small but elegant mansion revealing the same simple but clever taste that became known as Biedermeier across the Atlantic. But the Brett house, unusually, not only has its own garden surrounded by a wall, but also garden furniture, 47 pots with plants, outhouses that include a laundry and an outside three-seater privy (the Reverend Brett was obviously not too squeamish).

The house also has its own dolls: grandparents take their tea in the garden, a servant sweeps the garden and, of the two black servants, one nurses a baby in the bedroom. The furnishings include a fine collection of silver, mostly English or European though there is an American candlestick only 2cm (¾in) high. There are, too, tiny books, including a bible printed in 1780 and a 1786 "First Edition" of Burns's poems.

Because the furniture is either contemporary or (as it would be in a real house) earlier in date, the feeling of a family home is strong. Here is the harp for the mistress to play and a wedding chest belonging to an earlier generation, gros- and petit-point carpets, rag rugs (typically American) and a full complement of glass, porcelain and pictures. Even more charming is the tiny framed Brett coat of arms found in the dining room.

△ The real house of Sunnyside in Tarrytown on the Hudson River in New York State, has the same rambling early 18th-century elegance of Reverend Brett's dolls' house.

◁▽ The house opens up with the removal of separate sections of its front, one for each room. Each of the brick sections has sash windows and workable green shutters.

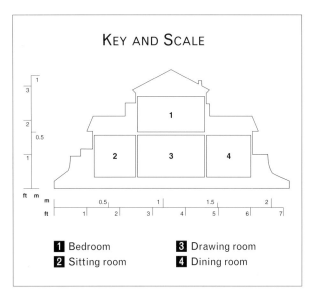

KEY AND SCALE

1 Bedroom
2 Sitting room
3 Drawing room
4 Dining room

DATE Made c.1838.
SCALE 91cm (3ft) high and 137cm (4 ft 6in) wide and 45cm (1ft 6in) deep.
STRUCTURE The whole is of simulated brick painted Indian red with small green workable shutters on the windows. The doors, both outside and in the rooms, have elegant arched fanlights and full-length French windows. One of the wings has a lacy "ironwork" porch and sitting-out area. The house has a central section consisting of two and a half storeys, as well as two single-storey wings. The attic half-storey, however, is for appearance only, so the house actually consists of only four main rooms plus a staircase hall and a basement.
LAYOUT OF ROOMS The house stands in its own garden. On the ground floor, the three rooms all interconnect. Behind a door in the dining room, a staircase rises to the single upper bedroom.

▷ The interior of Reverend Brett's house cleverly incorporates two single-storey wings although the attic is for appearance only. This house has a garden, where the grandparents are found having tea, and a conservatory.

◁ Detailing in the house is extraordinary: here is a tiny globe of the world made of pâpier-maché, an ivory lamp with glass globe fitting and two miniature powder horns.

▽ This painted wooden chest, decorated with typically American country scenes, dates from around 1753, 90 years earlier than the house and was probably owned by Lois Sexton of Somers, Connecticut.

◁ The Brett house is full of silverware suitable for a prosperous merchant family. Some are hall-marked and come from Britain and Europe as well as America. Pictured is a two-branch candelabra and a small tea urn with tap.

△ The harp is described in an inventory as "Sheraton carved black and gold laquer harp, serpentine valanced crest rail terminating on a reeded columnar standard." At 18cm (7⅛in) high, it has both strings and foot pedal. The music stand would be used by another musician in the family.

▷ This simple bookstand with three shelves and slanting top may be unique among dolls' house furniture though its style is similar to early 19th-century whatnots. On the top is a 1780 bible with, underneath, *Gray's Elegy,* a *history of England* and a dictionary.

△ Plumbing was in its infancy in early 19th-century New York, so this finely decorated tin water pump and wooden tub with washboard were necessary in the most elegant of houses. The pump's painting copies the very smart japanning of the period.

GERMAN TOYMAKERS

While Queen Victoria's dolls were little German Grödnertals, her dolls' house was not. It was a very simple inexpensive London-made "box back", similar to thousands made throughout the 19th century and later marketed by Silber & Fleming. Although the mass-production and world-wide sale of dolls' house furniture were quite advanced at this time, the houses were still made by small toymakers or carpenters. Curiously, while there are single miniature rooms, there are few German dolls' houses of the period in existence, although a large proportion of the furniture came from that country after the 1820s.

It was the wealthy German merchants of the early 19th century who began to organize the making of miniatures in wood, glass, tin and porcelain. These were then boxed in sets but without much information about where or how they had been made. We know, however, that in areas like Bohemia, there were factories employing a few men dotted all over the countryside. The workers were paid very little, living in extreme poverty and often made ill by the processes of manufacture – but the toys sold well because they were inexpensive.

They were perceived as cheap by their customers too. One Englishman, William Hewitt, writing in the mid-19th century, patronizingly said "Every article was totally foreign and queer. There were trumpets and wooden horses and rattles and swords and such like, but they would have made the children of England stare at their oddity. The toys were very strange and very cheap and of a primitive German air."

These miniature toys were not just playthings for German children; they were to teach little girls how to manage laundries and larders, kitchens and shopping. Women, from childhood onwards, were intended to devote their lives for the good of their families. W.H. Riehl, writing in 1854, crassly

added that women who wanted to spread their wings and, for example, become authors, were undoubtedly "ugly, soured and bitter". Not good enough, in fact, to marry and sink into domestic bliss.

To be fair, another German, Friedrich Froebel, was preaching a very different doctrine at the time. His view was that children were born with an innate tendency to work and to create and that strict methods of teaching were wrong. He founded the first Froebel Institute in 1813 and the first kindergarten in 1837, but the Prussian State considered his ideas so dangerous that these were later closed down.

THE TOY CATALOGUES

It was the German invention of catalogues (or master books) which really gave the country world pre-eminence in toy-making until the First World War, as well as the fact that the Germans took their toy-making seriously. The idea of putting the toys made individually by out-workers into a general catalogue from which the retail shops could order created a choice that was later to result from mass-production. The catalogues were lavish and beautifully hand-coloured (see opposite). They offered a huge choice of different designs and materials, and the wholesalers were able to direct the workers towards the most profitable lines.

One of the first German catalogues of dolls' house and other toys appeared in 1803 and 1807 from Georg Hieronymus Bestelmeier of Nuremberg, who was already exporting overseas before 1800. In the charmingly illustrated books, there are no fewer than 1,200 entries including tiny tea tables set with handleless teacups and teapots, cabinets, sofas and little dolls doing the washing. Numerous tiny wire chandeliers came in a choice of large and small, ornate and simple.

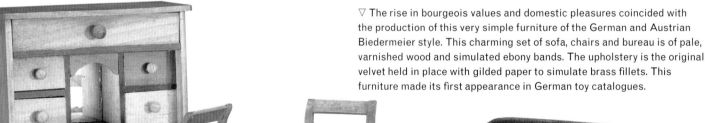

▽ The rise in bourgeois values and domestic pleasures coincided with the production of this very simple furniture of the German and Austrian Biedermeier style. This charming set of sofa, chairs and bureau is of pale, varnished wood and simulated ebony bands. The upholstery is the original velvet held in place with gilded paper to simulate brass fillets. This furniture made its first appearance in German toy catalogues.

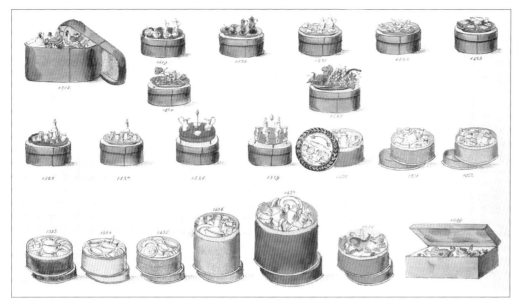

△ Although it is actually made of milk glass, painted with roses, this little box of crockery is clearly meant to imitate china which could not be worked into such tiny and fragile shapes. It is in its original German bentwood box and dates from c.1840.

◁ This page, from a Lindner toy catalogue c.1840, shows a selection of bentwood boxes full of china as seen above.

In Berchtesgaden, finely turned miniatures of ivory and bone had been made since the 17th century. The dolls' house historian Constance Eileen King notes that whole families were involved in the craft. Their skills were protected from outsiders, with sons being told family secrets only when their fathers lay dying. Others would be craftsmen in wood or tin until, around Christmas, they turned their skills towards making miniatures. Writing of a German sieve maker in the 1840s, William Hewitt says, with some poetic licence: "It was as if a magic spell had been exerted and all his tubs and barrels, sieves and spigots were converted into dolls, wooden boxes full of toys, chessboards and boards of other games. His tables were covered with boxes full of little household things, sets of kitchen utensils, little dinner services, whips and hobbyhorses, carts… churches and other buildings in sections for children to put together."

Waltershausen was another town in Germany which specialized in dolls and their furniture, with the firm Gebrüder Schneegas & Sohne becoming one of the most famous in the history of the creation of tiny furniture. It appeared in 1845 and made pieces in the Biedermeier style that was extremely popular all over northern Europe. The work was – and remained – of the highest quality (which is why it is so avidly collected), often featuring tiny turned spindles of bone and ivory.

BIEDERMEIER FOR DOLLS

The Biedermeier style lasted from the final defeat of Napoleon in 1815 until the middle of the 19th century. It was created for the bourgeoisie ("bieder" means plain and Meier was a very common German name) and praised their careful, modest ways – ways intended not to attract attention in a turbulent

▽ From Germany, this is a small-scale set of drawing room furniture. The original upholstery, in red, is typical of the 1840s period. The chair backs are of grained wood simulating rosewood and the upholstery is held to the frame with little gilt paper bands.

△ In the years before Victoria came to the throne house style in Britain, retained the lightness of the 18th-century furniture combined with the homeliness that came from the Biedermeier craze for blond wood and simple furnishings. The Shelton Taylor dolls' house, made in America in 1835, typifies the United States' version.

period of history. Professor Dr Wilhelm Mrazek, an expert on the period, says in the exhibition catalogue to *Vienna in the Age of Schubert* (Victoria & Albert Museum, 1979), "Great love and care was devoted to the creation of an intimate security and domesticity behind whose protective walls the individual could maintain his personal sense of identity and safely participate in the affairs of the world. Everything which belonged to the home and could be used in the house, everything small, useful, practical and economical, was cultivated."

Biedermeier style was homely with an unpretentious elegance and it was thought to mirror many of the virtues of the bourgoisie. Family musical evenings, family parties, games and unity were its ideal. The designs of furniture and interiors were never threatening: patterns were small, colours bright and clear with pale ceilings; and furniture was on a human scale. Chairs were arranged along the walls, pictures hung in simple lines above and the characteristic curvy sofa set behind a round table. In short, it was the ideal style for a dolls' house in an era when fashionable

ideas were transferring from grand houses in the country to the smart terraced city squares.

There is a typically Biedermeier dolls' house in the Simon van Gijn museum in Dordrecht, Holland. It dates from 1830 and is furnished with the characteristic light wooden furniture. Another example is the Shelton Taylor dolls' house (above) of 1835 in the Museum of the City of New York – demonstrating how far flung and popular the style was. Rooms have upright chairs, round pedestal tables and daybeds against the wall, while pictures, mostly family portraits, are kept to a minimum.

Another American house, the Cresson house (c.1810), was probably made for little Sarah Emlen Cresson, born in 1806. It is a symmetrical square block of a house, 18th-century English in inspiration, with very little of its original furniture intact. There are, however, two very nice, simple half tester beds, an American style adapted from English four-posters, while the downstairs fireplaces and adjoining cupboards, central hall and stairs and neatly panelled bedrooms have an appealing Biedermeier simplicity. A typical sofa of the period has also survived in the drawing room.

The American Voegler house, made by a Philadelphia cabinet maker in 1835, has a four-poster bed in a downstairs room (right). Its hangings and counterpane are made from handmade cotton lace; the original wallpaper is typically floral and small in scale. Upstairs, Biedermeier chairs with exaggerated top rails and sabre legs cluster around another round table.

This house was not made as a child's toy – it is 243cm (8ft) high – and was perhaps intended to demonstrate Mr Voegler's skill in cabinet making and upholstery. Either way, it mirrors exactly middle-class life in Philadelphia in the 1830s. It is both plain and elegant, uncluttered and sophisticated. The drawing room has a fine mirror over the fire and two good oil paintings on either side of it; a central table is covered with a decorative cloth and the windows with showy, swagged curtains. The dining room boasts another mirror over the fire and landscape wallpaper of the type that was being made in the great French factories. Even the kitchen is an area of calm: metal pots hang in ranks over the fire, a large square table acts as a work top and there is a rocking chair in the corner. The house also has a rare wash-stand made by a Philadelphia toy maker.

EVERYTHING UP TO THE MINUTE

In each case the dolls' houses are surprisingly up to the minute. Houses made between 1815 and 1840 leave no room for nostalgia. They are decorated and furnished throughout in the latest mode, not long after the latest mode appeared in real drawing and dining rooms. It is as if dolls' houses today were to be furnished by Tom Dixon and Philippe Starck and designed by Garouste and Bonetti or John Pawson.

But, as skills in mass-production advanced, manufacturers found it easier to stick with the same old models – and perhaps their young clients began to enjoy sticking to the old ways. The Biedermeier sofa made by Schneegas in the 1840s, when it was already starting to lose smartness, continued to be made for decades, as did the upright chairs with their sabre legs, even though the heavier straight-turned Victorian leg was fashionable by 1860. From now on, dolls' houses would gradually begin to lose their individuality. Neither the beautiful work of the skilled cabinet maker nor the bodging of the naive artist would survive the onset of inexpensive, readily available toys. But dolls' houses and their joys were at last beginning to reach children from less privileged families.

△ One of the most important mid-19th-century American houses was made in Philadelphia by a cabinet maker called Voegler. His intention was to display miniature examples of his furniture. The bed with lace hangings and the heavy chest of drawers (and pots under the bed) mirror real life in 1835.

▽ The Voegler house's drawing room features typical middle-class taste. This is a formal room with grandiose oil paintings, decorative silverware and a chimneypiece garniture. The pleasantly light and uncluttered wallpaper nonetheless makes it a delicate and light room.

▷ These houses are short on internal detail, so rooms can be designed as the owner wishes. This one lacks a dining room and, at the period, the house would have had a basement kitchen.

KEY AND SCALE

1 Bathroom
2 Nursery
3 Bedroom
4 Drawing room
5 Sitting room
6 Kitchen

DATE Made c.1830 although the furnishings have been added by the present owner.
SCALE 91cm (36in) high, 91cm (36in) wide, 33cm (13in) deep
STRUCTURE A plain wooden box painted a dark orange on the sides and back with darker bricks and stringing courses painted on the facade. The front doors have pilasters, fanlights, metal knockers and separate numbers. The chimneys are unusual in this style.
LAYOUT OF ROOMS Each "house" has three rooms over three storeys; there are no stairs. The top floor, designed by present owner, has a nursery and room with a tin bath. The first floor holds a bedroom and drawing room and the ground floor a kitchen and sitting room.

STAFFORD HOUSE

Simple dolls' houses like this one (known as Stafford house) are generally known as Silber & Fleming houses after the London firm of wholesalers who distributed them between 1850 and 1900. But this particular version is earlier in style and may, therefore, have preceded the company. The typical Silber & Fleming house is extremely simple with a box back without embellishment. The facade opens to reveal a series of plain rooms without stairs.

This dolls' house is designed like a pair of London terraced houses of around 1820. The probability is they were made for two sisters. Houses like this can be seen all over London with the characteristic black front door (here numbers 1 and 2) and decorated fanlight above. The ground floor windows are little more than half the size of the grand full-length affairs of the *piano nobile* which give maximum light in a city street, while the top floor windows are unpretentious. Above is a typical parapet hiding the slate roof.

Queen Victoria played with a similar dolls' house which, although straightforward in design, was fashionable in style as it was made at exactly the same time as such real houses were built.

▷ Terraces like these sprang up all over Britain's towns and cities from the 1780s to the end of the Regency period. Stafford house has copied the typical pedimented front door, the grand first floor windows surmounted by small servants' rooms and a plain pediment.

◁ Great care has been used on the front doors, which have lacy fanlights, solid furniture and pilasters. They are typical of early 19th-century English towns.

▷ The fireplaces indicate the grandeur of the rooms. This fashionable gothick arch appears in both first floor rooms. The wallpaper is probably contemporary with the house.

In the mid-19th century, American and European architectural styles were similar. The dolls' house known as the Thorndike Mansion (c.1850) is American but could mistaken for an English house. The Massachusetts street scene shows how such houses benefitted from the American sense of space, along with simple brick frontages and plain window surrounds.

CHAPTER FOUR

Early Victorian Values

1840–1860

In a period of extraordinary change, movement in architectural style took second place to building new towns. The industrial revolution saw a huge increase in the size of towns with basic terraces flung up to house the factory workers. Just as machines and homes were born out of the new industrial age, so were toys. Germany, which saw toys as educational, was the first country to use mass-production techniques for making toys and dolls' houses. This led to the country's pre-eminence in the field for half a century.

There are rare periods of history when one era can almost be seem to die and another take its place. In the early Victorian age, from 1840 to 1860, the 18th century, the age of reason and enlightenment, finally gave way to the 19th, the age of industrialization, mass-production and Empire. The same two decades also saw Queen Victoria, Empress of India, at her most revolutionary and vigorous. She ascended the throne in 1837 and with her marriage to Prince Albert in 1840, established an extraordinarily successful personal and political partnership. Among their achievements were the establishment of the Victoria & Albert Museum in London, and Great Exhibition held in London in 1851.

This was an era of enormous change and, as ever, dolls' houses mirrored these upheavals in their own quiet way. At the start of 1840, the carpenter dolls' house was supreme; by 1860 the market had begun to change, even though country families still had large dolls' houses made especially for them by skilled carpenters (see the carpenter-made dolls' house below).

However, the availability of mass-produced dolls' houses was not surprising. Machines were taking over virtually every area of life. A paddle steamer with 94 passengers had crossed the Atlantic in 19 days; the first proper bicycle could be seen in the streets along with the first steam omnibus; railways and the Houses of Parliament were being built even if the states of Texas and California were still to be born.

GAS STOVES AND SEWING MACHINES

In people's homes, an area which was quickly translated into dolls' houses, candles were still in use in the country but smart town houses were burning colza oil by the late 1830s, with

▷ Kitchens are frequently the most detailed rooms of a dolls' house, perhaps because the toy was also a learning aid and young women in Northern Europe were expected to be expert in all domestic crafts. This one, known as Holly Trees house (in the Holly Trees Museum, Colchester), has a black range (by Evans & Cartwright), fairly new for the period, earlier warming pan and bellows and a rustic dresser hung with plates and pewter. The clock and central table are of an earlier date – and the grocery basket is almost as big as the dolls.

△ James Lees-Milne, talent-spotting for the National Trust in England in the 1950s, discovered this carpenter-made house at Elsing Hall in Norfolk, then in the hands of two old ladies. He described it as Georgian style, with a drawer in the base and a roof that could be lifted off by its handle.

▷ This early, rare set of furniture dates from around 1840 and is probably English. The "wall climber" piano opens its rolltop to reveal paper keys. The rosette of fabric above is of purple silk, matching the music stool and the chiffonier. There is also a brown velvet daybed and matching chair.

paraffin to follow in 1853; gas lighting and heating was in its infancy – it was used for street lights around 1810 – but, by the Great Exhibition of 1851, gas cookers had been invented. Also in 1851, the first Singer sewing machine was making life easier for dressmakers and seamstresses, who had been sewing everything by hand with steel needles that had been invented 200 years before.

All this change was mirrored first in Victorian style and architecture and subsequently in the dolls' houses and dolls' house furniture of the time. Fashion, said regretful conservatives, had taken the place of tradition. Where once architects designed buildings that evolved in style, taking ancient classical and gothic examples for inspiration, now they cast about for ideas all over the world. Fuelled by Walter Scott's novels, romanticism was the essential element in creating the 19th-century tide of castles and abbeys from Bavaria to Brooklyn and there was Gothick, Egyptian and Chinese as exemplified by the Prince Regent's Royal Pavilion at Brighton.

On the other hand, the period saw the rise of the slums, back-to-back houses that were 3.3m (11ft) wide, 3.5m (11ft 6in) from back to front, at a density of 51.4 per hectare (127 per acre). The upper classes lived in spacious houses, the poor were so closely packed that infection jumped quickly between them. London had its frightening pea-soup fogs, caused by huge numbers of coal ranges used for cooking in every modern kitchen. At full blast, a single range could burn up to 15 scuttles of greasy coal every day – producing fogs in which six tons of soot mixed with the "air" over a mere square mile of the city. (Dolls' houses were fitted with similar ranges as can be seen in the kitchen of the Holly Trees house below.)

Not surprisingly, because industrial centres everywhere were similar, people all over Europe were emigrating to the wide, clean spaces of The United States in droves – mostly what Cobbett called "the sensible fellows", such craftsmen like wheelwrights, carpenters, smiths and bricklayers, who were sorely missed.

A NEW YORK BROWNSTONE

The brownstone buildings of New York are as famous as the Georgian brick terraces of London and the pale stone town houses of Paris. The typical brownstone house was exactly that: a mid-19th-century town house made of an iron-rich (and therefore rusty looking) stone. The architecture of the houses, which are generally in terraces, is a typical mid-19th-century version of the classical Palladian style.

Ornament is at a minimum, even for this period, with only the window surrounds, cornice and front door having classical detailing. The doors, however, are grand affairs; they are double, made in heavy wood with a strong surround and placed slightly above the street level, so they need an imposing set of stairs.

At this period, the first plate glass was appearing. However, this dolls' house still has the small panes and narrow glazing bars of the early 19th century combined with the heavy windows of mid-century, which dates it to c.1850. It is an exact replica of a real brownstone that has since been demolished.

The wallpapers are very elaborate, with a block-print paper designed to look like cane in the bedroom and, in the grand salon below, one of the fashionable landscape-papered rooms with a heavy gilded cornice. A *tour de force*, this painting is actually on canvas, signed 1853 – although in real life, landscape papers were imported from France and papered to the walls. The papers of the ground floor – a dark green stripe with gilded motif and a snuff-brown paper with high cream gothic arches – are equally fashionable. It is furnished with beautiful and rare Biedermeier-style furniture originally bought by a young girl from Massachusetts in 1850. The present owner bought it four years ago for just this house.

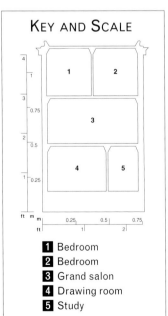

◁ New York, like major cities the world over, started expanding in the early 19th century, when the fashionable Palladian style created rows of disciplined terraces like these brownstones. Both they and the dolls' house version rely on stairs to an upper ground floor and front door to light the semi-basement. The window treatments of both are heavy and effective when massed in terraces.

DATE Made c.1850.
SCALE 138cm (54in) high, 79cm (31in) wide, 41cm (16in) deep.
STRUCTURE Carpenter-built from wood that has been painted to imitate iron-rich, brownstone. The house is flat-fronted with an ornamental cornice hiding the shallow roof behind it. The windows on the ground floor vary in size compared to the first and second floor windows, but they are all the same width and are glazed with real glass. The dolls' house has double mahogany front doors placed slightly above street level at one side of the building, as was usual with real brownstone houses, and an imposing set of stairs lead from the street to the house.
LAYOUT OF ROOMS The three-storey house comprises five rooms; it has no staircase and the windows do not really correspond to the simple rooms which are, however, extremely grandly furnished with not a kitchen in sight.

KEY AND SCALE

1 Bedroom
2 Bedroom
3 Grand salon
4 Drawing room
5 Study

◁ As well as the extremely grand wallpapers the house contains equally grand chandeliers, a faux marble fireplace and carefully created cornices. The dolls are very grand too.

▷ At the period, all sorts of odd materials were used to make pictures – feathers, shells and, here, cork. This is a faux cork dolls' house picture with a pressed paper mount and green gilded frame.

▽ White Biedermeier furniture for dolls' houses is extremely rare, although very suitable in its light colouring. This charming sewing table has tiny compartments for silks, cottons and needles, while the winged armchair has a matching footstool. Both are elegantly painted and are part of a large set of furniture found in the ground floor rooms.

▷ "Blackamoor" servants, exotically dressed in brilliant satins, turbans and gold braid, were popular from the 16th century, where they often appear in portraits. This little servant boy (there is larger, gaudily dressed black servant in the house too) would not be expected to do manual work (his clothes are hardly suitable) but amuse and carry for his mistress.

◁ This rare furniture from Waltershausen in Germany is in transition from Regency to Victorian. The over-stuffed chair, upholstered in pale blue silk and gold braid, is decorated with pressed metal to look like ormolu, as is the neat chest of drawers. They are very decorative and made to look like French metal-trimmed furniture.

◁ This ornate, five-light oil lamp is one of many table lights and hanging lights in the house and is made from enamelled metal. Oil lamps were a 19th-century innovation which allowed light to be positioned for sewing and eating.

VICTORIA AND FAMILY VALUES

If Queen Victoria and Prince Albert (and their relations who reigned all over Europe) had a great, but diffused, role in the creation of 19th-century values, they had rather more direct influence on family values. Victoria was the first queen on the British throne in over 100 years and, unlike Queen Anne, her many children lived. She was fertile, she was motherly, she had advanced views on bringing up children. She was given "that blessed chloroform" on the birth of her eighth child in 1853, only six years after its first use. Albert was a highly domestic consort with an interest in architecture. He even felt moved to design some model houses for the poor – four dwellings to a building, each having a general room cum kitchen, two small bedrooms to segregate the boys from the girls, a large bedroom for the parents and babies, plus a scullery and lavatory. Each room had a cupboard and each dwelling a water supply. For the first time, general cleanliness came second only to godliness.

Even artisans' houses in the 1850s could be charming and cosy, far from the Dickensian idea of the lower classes' homes. An account in 1850 of a cabinet-maker's house describes "the warm red glow of the mahogany furniture, a clean carpet covers the floor; a few engravings in neat frames hang against the papered wall; and bookshelves or a bookcase have their appropriate furniture. Very white and bright-coloured pot ornaments, with sometimes a few roses in a small vase, are reflected in a mirror over the mantelpiece." It could be describing the living room of a dolls' house of the period like the two- sided dolls' house shown here. For instance, the top left-hand living room (far right illustration) has nearly all of the above attributes, including a "a few roses in a small vases".

This modest little house, known as Villa Lily, was made in Scandinavia around 1860. From one side it has a simple set of four rooms and a hall for one child to play while the other side

▷▽ Dolls of the period saw cleanliness as next to godliness. Here, with some variations in scale, an 1850s tinplate two-seater shower, bath, hot water can, two children in tubs to be put before the nursery fire and lastly a large basin and ewer.

△ Villa Lily is a Scandinavian one-off house made by a carpenter around 1860. It has a typically Northern European gabled roof, detailed with diaper tiles, which has its own attic room. The house is unusual in that it opens on both sides, allowing two children to play with it. It is by no means an accurate model; the stairs do not seem to go anywhere and the chimneys do not match up with the fires. However, the patterned wallpaper is made to scale and is very much in tune with the times. The furniture is German.

follows the same pattern but with a garret room in the roof. The whole stands on a painted wooden base simulating a stable (not shown). Although it is furnished throughout with German pieces from Waltershausen, including a cherry wood dining set upholstered in pale blue, the atmosphere is definitely Scandinavian, perhaps because of the charming patterned wallpapers. Although Germany monopolized the world-wide dolls' house trade, they adapted designs to suit the tastes and styles of their different markets.

"EVERY MORNING I DRESS MY DOLL"

Victoria had seen many changes occur. She had been brought up in comparative poverty for a Royal and, as previously mentioned, actually had a dolls' house of her own. Far from being a baby palace, it was a modest, two-roomer with a typical townhouse frontage of the early 19th century.

Later in life Victoria was regularly to give dolls' houses to other children. Princess Charlotte of Belgium was one, for we know she wrote in 1848 to thank her cousin for the present: "I have received the beautiful dolls' house you have been so kind to send me and I thank you very much for it. I am delighted with it; every morning I dress my doll and give her a good breakfast; and the day after her arrival she gave a great rout at which all my dolls were invited. Sometimes she plays at drafts on her pretty little draft-board, and every evening I undress her and put her to bed."

A decade later, a more modest little girl – 10-year-old Mary Eliza Joy – described Rose Villa: "About a month ago it was an

△ A very large, carpenter-made dolls' house makes an ideal plaything for a little girl. Its rooms are very spacious and the plate-glass windows all open, including those at the back. Although the fanlight is typically Georgian, this house dates from the mid-19th century. Inside there are four large rooms and a central hall on the ground floor with stairs leading up to a landing with an arched window.

◁ The bedroom from the dolls' house above has its original floral-sprigged wallpaper, a half-tester bed with original hangings (dwarfed by the enormous window) and a floral printed *chaise longue* with matching chairs and pouffes. The high ceilings of the rooms allow easy access for children's hands.

old square box with no lid; at last papa wrote to the carpenter desiring him to come to our house. Well he came and mama told him what to do. It was made into partitions so that there were four rooms in it, kitchen, the parlour, drawing room and a bedroom. We papered it ourselves, the parlour with light green, the bedroom a white ground with the outlines of ivy leaves in pink colour." [The bedroom from the house shown opposite has similar wallpaper only the flowers are blue on a white background.] "The drawing room is papered with a pale blush pink colour, imitating watered silk. The kitchen is not papered at all, for we had nothing now (nor had we then) to paper it with… Grandmama Spratt bought us a great boxful of furniture, besides the drawing room chairs which I carved and covered myself and the box of kitchen things I have had for years. She also brought us a little box of tea things and I do not think I ever saw any so pretty. They are made of glass and (I believe) painted white on the side to imitate china. And on the outside are painted bouquets of forget-me-nots and a few green leaves…" (as seen on page 67).

The extent to which families furnished and looked after their dolls' houses is epitomized by the Warren house made in Salem, Massachusetts, by a cabinet maker for the four daughters of Mrs J. Mason Warren in 1852. It is 183cm (6ft) high and 51cm (20in) deep with eight rooms and a hall. Almost everything which can be is marked with a tiny W – it is embroidered on tablecloth and napkins in the pantry and sheets and pillowcases in the bedroom. Inside a desk in the dining room is a "walnut shell with white gloves enclosed which was handed to Mrs Warren at her engagement dinner." (Gloves, given as gifts, were seen as a declaration of love at this time.)

More interesting still is the drop-leaf mahogany dining table which is supposed to have been made of wood from a British ship captured in 1812 by the privateer, *America*, owned by the Crowninshield family, Mrs. Warren's maiden name. The tiny table was apparently part of a set of toys being sent to an Empire family in India.

The library was a copy of the real Warren house in Boston which was demolished in about 1876. There are oak bookcases on either side of the fireplace, their lack of books hidden by red silk curtains. There's a fire with coal in it and a little square piano. In the centre of the room, a round table has tiny cards arrayed on it and miniature books in French. A games table in the same room has minute chessmen. The

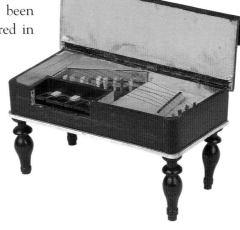

△ Music was a preoccupation in Victorian households and in dolls' houses too. This square piano is by Schneegas at Waltershausen. The lid is fully back revealing a green lining and showing how the mechanism is made. It would actually play a tinny tune but is no more than 15cm (6in) long.

black servant doll has her own sofa in the kitchen as well as scrubbing brush, clothes horse and water pump.

Large houses with rooms almost big enough to hold a small child playing with her dolls were also being made in Europe. The English house opposite with its post-1840s plate-glass windows, is the size of a chest of drawers and opens out to reveal four very spacious rooms. Its door and fanlight are rather old-fashioned for the date but give a pleasant classical look to a carpenter-made toy.

THE NEW NURSERY

In the mid-19th century, nurseries – rooms that were the children's realm – became important for the first time. Whereas 18th-century children were stuffed away in badly ventilated attics where the furniture tended to be household cast-offs, the well-to-do Victorian child had a proper nursery and proper toys. The style sped quickly around the world, encouraged by those prim English governesses that grand families as far afield as Russia felt they had to employ.

Girls whose families could afford it were generally taught by governesses but boys went to school, where the carrot of enjoyment of learning was beginning to overtake the stick of punishment. Girls learnt enough to cope with adult life – arithmetic to deal with household accounts, history and literature to provide adequate conversation and a little French or Italian along with the polite arts of music, sketching and needlework. When aged less than 10 years old they were making laborious samplers with improving mottoes so working on dolls' house linen and tiny carpets was far more enjoyable.

Queen Victoria may have remembered her favourite dolls' house toy when she began to change the world of children for ever. When Osborne, her holiday home on the Isle of Wight, was being built, the nurseries were carefully placed on the second floor so that she and Albert could visit the growing brood. In creating cosy rooms for her children, Victoria was copying notions that came from less grand families. Albert, too, must have been influenced by the deliberately unpretentious German Biedermeier style which emphasized the virtues of domesticity and intimacy among the family. Meanwhile, in the United States, where the pioneers were still struggling westward, parents were bringing up their children with Puritan spareness, making furniture and toys especially for them.

A New York Mansion

◁ The entrance hall has a hand-painted floor made to look like tiles. A group of dogs seem perfectly at home here. At the back of the hall there is a bird cage by Rock & Gräner. The coachman, dressed in his original uniform, prepares to take the luggage upstairs. All of the dolls in the house are contemporary with the period.

◁ The lithophane was one of many 19th-century inventions to disappear. Carved porcelain was held up in screens and lit from behind by a candle to give a realistic, if monochrome, picture. These two dolls' house versions include a fire screen which would be lit by embers instead of candle flames.

▷ Dolls did not just have birds, dogs and monkeys as pets – they had squirrels. This black and gold painted metal cage by Rock & Gräner is most decorative although highly uncomfortable for the squirrel.

◁ Dolls' furniture-makers took to chromolithography with zeal. Here Schneegas at Waltershausen have put a classical landscape and flower painting on the seat and back of a mid-19th century chair. The complete set is in the bottom, left-hand room.

◁ Running water was not common in many houses even during the second half of the 19th century. Various devices were invented to make fresh water regularly available for washing and drinking. This tiny version has a small, brass tap and hanging jug.

△ Pity the giant goldfish confined to this small bowl on its gilded stand. Fish, dogs, parrots and other pets turn up in dolls' houses of this period – see also the squirrel cage on the right.

▷ An early version of the hostess trolley, by Rock & Gräner. This tiny dining-room toy comes complete with a huge ham in a decorative pastry crust complete with surrounding vegetables. Its wheels actually turn.

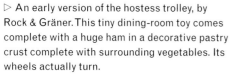

△The intricacy of tiny dolls' house furniture is extraordinary. This foldaway baby bath (by Rock & Gräner) can be pulled out at washtime and hidden all day. The faux marble top would be the changing area and the bottom drawer holds nappies and other supplies. The bath is not plumbed but has a little bucket for hot water before and slops after.

▷ Although the kitchen is not too cluttered, it has much in common with the early 16th-century German dolls' houses – the hand-painted tiled floor, displays of plates and quantities of baskets. The black bisque servant dolls are dressed in their original matching uniforms.

Victoria was not the only European princess to play with a dolls' house. The famous Three Sisters house (shown on the opposite page), now in the Nationalmuseet in Copenhagen, was made around 1850 for the Danish royal family and has the cipher of Crown Prince Frederick VIII to prove it. The three sisters who played in its three storeys were the little Princesses Ingeborg, Thyra and Dagmar.

Victorian style with a Swedish twist appears in the Emily Kihlberg house (below right) of six rooms which dates from about 1856. It was furnished and arranged by Mrs Kihlberg for her 10 children and three step-children. The story goes that they were only allowed to look in with their hands behind their backs – chaos and fighting would otherwise ensue. The symmetrical arrangements of chairs, mirrors and pictures along with the voile curtains and warmly-wrapped dolls are typically Scandinavian. Typically Northern European, too, is the single room pavilion (below) known as Anna's Pleasure. Sweden is dotted with these little summer, lake or fishing houses where families would come on all-too-rare summers' days. It, too, has the fine voile curtains and symmetrical style.

ENGLISH TOYMAKERS

At first, before the German toymakers had established the virtual monopoly that they achieved between the mid-19th century and the First World War, there were plenty of English toymakers about. In 1841, according to Mayhew, there were 407 toymakers and 146 toy merchants in London alone. These would include turners, greenwood and white wood toymakers, fancy toymakers or modellers and two varieties of doll maker, one making wooden and the other sewn dolls. Toys were also made in tin, lead and pewter. There were specialists called "Bristol" toymakers who had originally come from the city but now simply specialized in making cheap toys for the comparatively poor at a penny a time which contradicts the notion that the lower classes were bereft of all but necessities. Because these toys were so inexpensive, few have survived.

△ Anna's Pleasure is an exquisite one-room wooden summer house from Sweden or Denmark, where city folk often built single-room pleasure pavilions on the many lakes. It is furnished in the spare but elegant style associated with Sweden – rich but plain curtains on poles, soft, greenish-grey walls, a curly-backed sofa and glass chandelier. A low table is set with a silver coffee set. The rocking chair and cradle are rather more rustic.

▷ Emily Kihlberg organized this busy Swedish house around 1856 for her 10 children and three step-children. Emily herself really enjoyed creating the rooms with gilded but simple walls, lacy curtains, carefully arranged small pictures and dolls warmly wrapped against the cold. The kitchen is hardly changed from those in 16th-century German houses.

▷▷ The Three Sisters house (far right), dating from 1850, was the toy of Princesses Ingeborg, Dagmar and Thyra of Denmark. The grand drawing room is in the simple Biedermeier style but with Scandinavian touches like the white clock and furniture.

It is, predictably, from Charles Dickens that we have the most colourful description of toymakers of the time. In *Cricket on the Hearth*, published in 1845, he writes about Caleb, the poor toymaker. "Caleb and his daughter were at work together in their usual working room, which served them for their ordinary living room as well… There were houses in it, finished and unfinished, for dolls of all stations in life. Suburban tenements for dolls of moderate means, kitchen and single apartments for dolls of the lower classes; capital town residences for dolls of high estate. Some of these establishments were already furnished according to estimate, with a view to the convenience of dolls of limited income; others could be filled on the most expensive scale… from whole shelves of chairs and tables, sofas, bedstead and upholstery. The nobility and gentry and public in general, for whose accommodation these tenements were designed, lay, here and there in baskets, staring straight up at the ceiling; but in denoting their degree of society and confining them to their respective stations (which experience shows to be lamentably difficult in real life) the makers of the dolls had far improved on nature, which is often forward and perverse; for they, not resting on such arbitrary marks as satin, cotton, print and bits of rag, had… striking personal differences which allowed no mistake."

Some toymakers, like Caleb, were virtual department stores for dolls' houses, providing the house itself, whether terrace or palace, the furniture in all grades of expense and the dolls to match. Others specialized in cheap pieces made from pine. In 1852, for instance, such a toymaker explained his work: "In sawn and plain pinewood, I manufacture penny and halfpenny toy bellows, penny and halfpenny toy tables, penny wash-hand stands, chiefly for Baby Houses, penny dressers with drawers for the same purpose, penny bedsteads. The toy bellows now have no run. Six or seven years ago there was a great rage for them. Then I made about twelve thousand in one year but you see they were dangerous and induced children to play with fire, so they soon went out of fashion."

Henry Mayhew (best known for his social survey *London Labour and the London Poor*) also describes a toymaker in Bethnal Green, London: "I found a cripple himself in bed but still sitting up, with a small desk-like bench before him." He cut, from pinewood, little pieces which would be sold by the warehouses in Sheffield and Birmingham for less than a penny. The whole family helped, especially a daughter who was highly skilled. All the family, although poor, could read and write.

Then, as now, the magazines were encouraging their readers to try their own hands at making dolls' houses and furniture.

◁ Some early American furniture, made in cast iron probably either by George W. Brown or J. and E. Stevens of Connecticut. The little chair and sofa are more ornate than they would be in a real drawing room.

◁ A Danish cupboard house – one without an architectural front – dating from around 1850. The main room's curtains are charmingly light and airy in Scandinavian style while the kitchen has rustic lace. The kitchen floor is tiled and the dresser hung with plates. There are oil lamps and an oil hanging light in the drawing room. Much of the furniture is German and later, and there is a rare Evans & Cartwright sofa.

▷ The kitchen always helps date a house because this is where new inventions first appear. This one (from the house on page 80) has warming ovens on the right which would be stuffed with hot coals. The sink has a water tank above. There is a rack for spits above the iron range.

△ A tiny kettle of remarkable quality from the above kitchen. The lid lifts off and there is no doubt that water could be boiled in it. It is probably English and may even come from the London maker of copper dolls' house equipment whom Henry Mayhew interviewed in the mid-19th century.

Hence, the *Girls's Own Toymaker*, in 1859, was giving its young readers instructions on how to make model houses and cottages for ornaments in the real drawing room. While dolls' houses were, increasingly, seen as playthings for young children, and thus expendable, the old idea of the smart show-case was still around. It was interesting, too, that model-making was considered suitable for girls, which was not the case earlier in the century.

In the United States the firm of Francis, Field and Francis were making tin toys in Philadelphia from 1848. They used early mass-production methods to make tin clocks, chairs, bureaux and other furniture for "a gentle girl to establish in her own dolls' house".

TINY COPPER KETTLES

Henry Mayhew also visited a London maker of copper toys, pieces that would have been accessories around the hearth. Talking in 1845, the man revealed that he had worked in the trade from the age of five, helping his father clean the toys: "At present, I make chiefly copper tea-kettles, coffee-pots, coal scuttles, warming pans and brass scales, these are the most run on, but I make besides brass and copper hammers, saucepans, fish kettles and other things." It needed 16 pieces to make a single toy tea kettle – the handle in three pieces, seven for the top and cover, two for the spout, one for the bottom, a single piece for the side and two rivets to fix the handle – "That's the portion of the trade requiring the most art."

"Copper toys are the hardest work… of any toy work. The copper is this dull sheet of copper here, 8 feet square is the sheet of it. I use generally a 4-pound sheet costing 13 pence a pound. I make six dozen tea-kettles out of one sheet." In a week, he could make around a hundred such kettles. "I make all that is made in London, yes, in the world. Here's the world's shop, sir, this little place, for copper toys. I make as many scuttles in a week as I do tea-kettles… and as many coffee-pots. They're all fit to boil water in, cook anything you like, every one of them. They are made on exactly the same principle as the large kettles except that they are brazed together and mine are soft soldered." These miniature miracles cost sixpence each.

Working away in his little workshop, this toymaker seemed to think he was virtually alone in the world but he was sadly ill-informed. The toymakers of Germany were starting to take over the trade all over Europe by creating mass-production factories that would put the single craftsman out of business.

By the second half of the 19th century, American architecture was beginning to mix its European influences. This dolls' house from Boston (c.1880) has both a cupola and mansard roof plus French double entrance doors. The background buildings of real Boston show the same mix of influences.

CHAPTER FIVE

Mid-Victorian Opulence
1860–1880

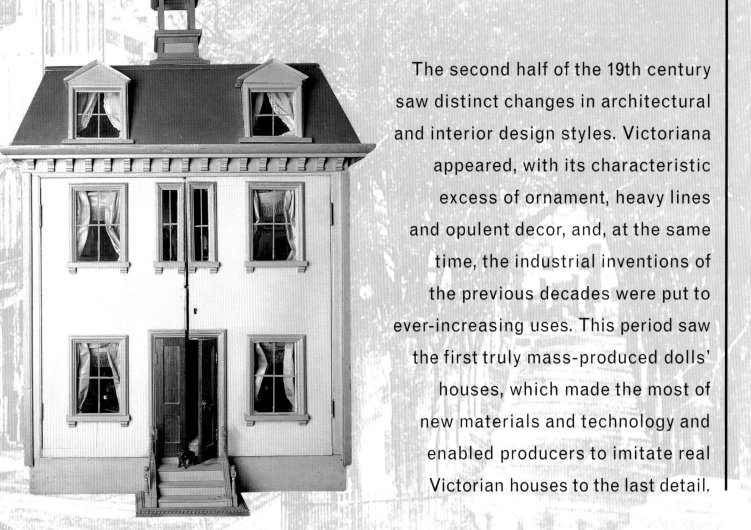

The second half of the 19th century saw distinct changes in architectural and interior design styles. Victoriana appeared, with its characteristic excess of ornament, heavy lines and opulent decor, and, at the same time, the industrial inventions of the previous decades were put to ever-increasing uses. This period saw the first truly mass-produced dolls' houses, which made the most of new materials and technology and enabled producers to imitate real Victorian houses to the last detail.

Mrs Beeton, in her world-famous book, *Household Management*, which first came out in 1861, noted a change in looking after children. "The children's hour," she wrote bossily, "should be an institution in every household and, while to the young folks it should be the happiest time of the day, to the attendants (i.e. nannies, nursemaids and servants) it is a great rest and relief. Let the children then bring their little troubles and sorrows to mother to be set right and comforted... she will not find an hour wasted in this way, even if it be one hard to spare."

One great change that happened throughout the 19th century was that children were treated less like little adults and more like children. They were not expected to amuse themselves with simple things like hoops and tops but, in the middle class at any rate, grew up in nurseries full of toys and looked after by servants.

The story behind the American dolls' house, shown right, tells of one such lucky young girl, who was more than likely looked after by servants but who also had a doting mother.

The house is well-documented and unusual in that it has both a name and a date. Bessie Mitchell's dolls' house was given to her at Christmas in 1879 when she was eight years old. It was made by a carpenter employed by her grandfather and furnished by her doting mother. As Flora Gill Jacob notes, "it was no mere store-bought house 'fitted up' at a local toy shop" and a great deal of love and imagination went into making it.

▷ The interior of Bessie Mitchell's dolls' house includes a mixture of Biedermeier furniture imported from Germany and American Bliss furniture. The wallpapers, handmade curtains and drapes, Victorian pictures in homemade frames and Japanese fans are all original.

Although Bessie Mitchell's house was carpenter-made, the furniture inside was mostly commercially produced. Toys were beginning to be mass-produced and, as Mrs Beeton noticed, "In spite of the fact that children have far more... toys with every advancing year... it is just as difficult to amuse them as it ever was. She goes on to make the point that children like to help create their own toys: "Playthings are often too complete when given to children. Dolls are dressed... horses are harnessed, dolls' houses as well fitted as real ones, so that there is nothing left to be done by the little ones to whom contriving and making are pleasures in themselves."

SEEN AND NOT HEARD

Despite the sentimental tone of Mrs Beeton's writing, children in the Victorian home did not have a particularly jolly time. While maxims like "Spare the Rod and Spoil the Child" and "Children Should be Seen and Not Heard" are constantly mentioned in books on the period, they have the ring of the dog training manual about them – wishful thinking. In the fourth volume of their book, *A History of Everyday Things in England*, published in 1934, the authors Marjorie and C.H.B Quennell comment: "We can remember very clearly our own grandmother's tales of family life in the sixties and how, as children, we listened with envy to her accounts of the freedom and comradeship enjoyed by a houseful of 15 lively boys and girls. The family in question was a very ordinary one, neither rich nor distinguished."

Parents were, however, severe. They expected their children always to obey, to be respectful and never answer back. Only during "children's hour" were they allowed to talk freely to their parents. Although they had many more toys than children in earlier centuries, the times they were allowed to play with them were strictly limited. There were regular family services, homework as well as full-time schooling from a governess – a fairly rich household would put aside two rooms for nurseries and a third for the schoolroom. On Sundays, toys and picture books (except, the Noah's Ark which came from a Bible story) were locked away, with improving texts taking their place. Games and music – apart from hymns – were forbidden, while dancing and cards were positively sinful. Nowhere, however, are there signs that piano legs had to be covered to preserve young people's modesty. This, it seems, was a later fable created to make the Victorians appear even more prudish than they were.

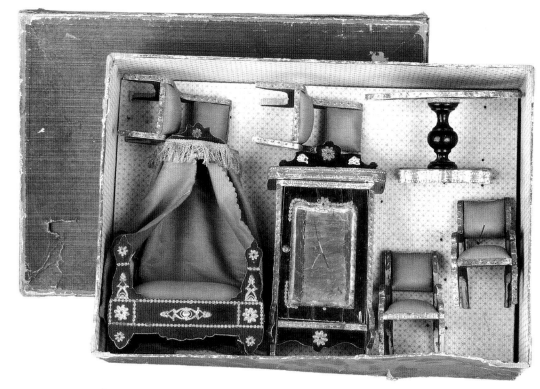

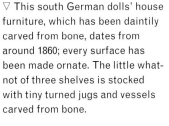

▽ This south German dolls' house furniture, which has been daintily carved from bone, dates from around 1860; every surface has been made ornate. The little what-not of three shelves is stocked with tiny turned jugs and vessels carved from bone.

△ In its original box – but probably missing a dressing table – this bedroom set comes from Germany. It is made of wood painted to look like rosewood, with embossed gold paper added as brass inlay. It dates from the late 1870s but has a near Empire simplicity of line, and may have been made for the French market. The set includes a handsome bed with hangings, four chairs, a pretty gilded table and a stout wardrobe and mirror. The upholstery is blue silk. German makers prided themselves on their packaging and the box is beautifully lined with patterned paper.

HIP BATHS AND HARD WORK

Although, in many ways, the Victorian house looks almost modern to our eyes – perhaps because the typical busy style became so fashionable a few years ago – everyday life was very different from today. New inventions were appearing all the time – a cable to America in 1864 and the telephone in 1876, for instance – but most of the technology missed the home.

Most homes did not have plumbed-in baths or special rooms to wash in for, apparently, our ancestors did not at all like the idea of sharing the same bath tub. Instead, hip baths were set up beside the fire and hot water ferried from the basement by a maid. The average middle-class household would probably have two or three maids to do most of the domestic work.

And there was a great deal of work to do in 19th-century homes. In towns, where most of the population now lived, most middle-class houses would have the kitchen and store rooms in the basement; the storeys in between would be for dining, living and entertaining, with the top floors given to the children and attics to the servants. Coal would have to be dragged up all the stairs from the coal hole under the street by the maids – and the ashes brought back down again. The washing of linen and clothes had to be done by hand with the aid of an old copper boiler and wrung out with a hand mangle.

The cook probably spent as much time preserving, bottling, making chutney and pickles, fruit cordials and vinegars as actually cooking meals. There was tinned food but it was generally only used on long sea voyages or by explorers because good plain cooks distrusted it and of course there was no refrigeration.

MASS PRODUCTION

However, as we all know from the neo-Victorian style so popular in more recent years (1970s), the house was absolutely crammed with objects. Every mantelpiece was crowded with figures, candlesticks, vases and glass domes with wax or glass flowers, stuffed birds and the like. There were embroidered

△ Clocks for dolls' houses come in the many styles of the real timepieces. The first clock is a very expensive dolls' toy, of gilded and embossed tin. Next is an unusual mantel clock made of black glass, followed by a tall tin standing clock with blue paper behind the pendulum; its hands and pendulum both move. Finally, there is another mantel clock in embossed metal. All are German and from the last quarter of the 19th century.

cushions and bell pulls, footstools and small mats, objects brought back by relatives who had returned from outposts of the Empire – elephant tusks, Benares brassware and African spears were all proudly displayed.

A good example of this clutter is the British carpenter-made Manor house (right), created for Alice Chater in 1854, although its furnishings were added to for many years. Tables groan with tea silver, oil-lamps and ewers are scattered in the bedroom and in the kitchen, where the butler appears to be listening to an old wireless, the mantle above the range is crowded with pots.

All this busy-ness was made possible by mass-production. Furniture, patterned fabrics and carpets, prints on the wall, decorative ceramics were now made by machine, not by hand. They were cheaper and more plentiful – and new. All, too, had been given Royal approval at the Great Exhibition of 1851, a riot of boasting, inventiveness and skill.

The Great Exhibition's god was mass-production and its creation was the work of Prince Albert, Victoria's Consort. It

◁ This American, cast-iron hip bath dates from about 1860, long before plumbed baths were generally used. It is reminiscent of those seen in Western films.

▷ Suitable for any Victorian dolls' house bedroom, this English washstand is of real mahogany with a ewer and basin plus soap stand. It dates from the 1860s. There are many pieces found made by the same maker whose name or firm has not yet been identified.

is said that he had to sweep away a great deal of scepticism and opposition when he first proposed it – but his views were vindicated by its huge success. But, although Britain was the greatest power in the world at that time, with its Empire, its trade and its huge, innovative factories, Albert's message that mass-production was king missed British toymakers but was heard loud and clear in Germany.

GERMAN DOMINATION

The worldwide trade in dolls' houses and furniture of the mid-19th century was utterly dominated by Germany. The houses, the dolls and the furniture all came from German makers, and

△ Made for Alice Chater in 1854, Manor House is a real mish-mash of styles, mostly of the last half of the 19th century. It is peopled with dandified male dolls, a complement of servants (one listening to an early wireless) plus a precocious child and glowing electric fire in the dining room.

even houses and furniture which look English, or French, or American were often German made, for the manufacturers had the sense to vary the styles of roof and front door, of chair and bed, of maid and mistress to suit the importing country. Things occasionally went wrong, of course, and mysteriously uniformed figures in English, French or American dolls' houses, taken to be butlers or visiting musicians, are actually German admirals.

A MID-VICTORIAN CARPENTER-MADE DOLLS' HOUSE

This carpenter-made house has been in the same Norfolk family since it was made in the 1870s. It was made for two sisters, Laura and Sybil. In style, it seems earlier than late 19th century – the classical sizes of the windows and heavy quoins seem late 18th century – but the only remaining glazing bar shows it once had plate-glass windows and therefore could not be earlier than the 1850s.

The house is very plain, especially inside, where there is no wallpaper but soft blue and buff paintwork instead. But it is a fully functional dolls' house. The stairs go right up three storeys, every door opens and each room has a fireplace with a "marble" surround. The kitchen fire "blazes".

One of the family who played with it as a child and put in new window glass in 1951, recalls "It was very satisfying to play with because everything works. It is very frustrating to children when things don't."

▷ The Georgian House, in Bristol, exemplifies the clean lines and simple proportions of mid-Georgian domestic taste. This is a detached town house, which originally probably belonged to a rich merchant. Its central doorway, similar-sized sash windows (the top storey being slightly smaller) and ashlar detailing are echoed in the dolls' house, even though it is much later.

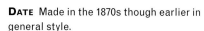
▷ The six-room dolls' house has a generous set of stairs with landings and doors which open with little bone handles. Each room has a fitted fireplace. The house is very solidly built.

DATE Made in the 1870s though earlier in general style.

SCALE 122cm (48in) high, 91cm (36in) wide, 43cm (17in) deep

STRUCTURE Carpenter-made of wood painted to look like ashlar blocks with corner quoins. The hinged doors open to the left of the front door which does not open. The roof lifts up to reveal an attic where spare and broken furniture may be stored. The whole stands on a low, cabriole-legged pedestal.

LAYOUT OF ROOMS There are three storeys with two rooms, hall and stairway on each storey. The ground floor has a dining room and a kitchen on either side of the hall; the first floor has a formal drawing room on the right and less formal sitting room on the left while on top there is a bedroom and night nursery.

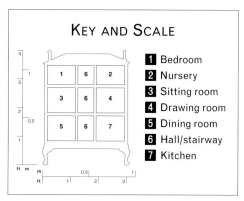

KEY AND SCALE

1 Bedroom
2 Nursery
3 Sitting room
4 Drawing room
5 Dining room
6 Hall/stairway
7 Kitchen

▽ A German bureau with marbled paper on the flap that lets down to reveal drawers. These actually open. This is probably one of the house's original pieces.

◁ A tiny set of German dinner china painted with violets. These were favourites of one owner who later found a lid to fit the 4cm (1½in) tureen. "It was very satisfying to lay the table", she recalls.

◁ In the late 19th century, people were still using hip baths in front of the bedroom fire. The housemaid would ferry the water from range to bath in such a hot water can. This one is less than 5cm (2in) high.

▷ More German furniture but clearly made in the English style. The dining room set includes chairs, table, chest of drawers and a cupboard made in a faux dark-red wood, clearly imitating the heavy mahogany furniture fashionable in the late 19th century. This set is contemporary with the house.

▷ The set of fire irons is unusual in that it is made of heavy cast iron. It is therefore probably English (German makers would have used a lighter, soft metal). The style suggests that the three pieces are original. They come from the drawing room.

◁ One category of mass-produced German dolls' houses, made over a long period of time, is known as blue roof houses – many of these were made by Gottschalk. (The roofs of both of these houses have been repainted). The ornate architectural details are printed chromo-lithographs glued to wood. One house (far left) has three ground floor windows; the other (left), only two. In front stands a pretty set of painted furniture, moulded in soft metal.

THE DOLLS' HOUSE MARKET

An article, published in the *Daily Telegraph* in 1875, exclaims: "The Germans excel in the construction of Lilliputian crockery, kitchen utensils and imitation fruits and viands. A wagon-load of such articles could be obtained from Houndsditch in half an hour and a dolls' house as big as a cabinet piano could be swiftly furnished."

While British toymakers continued as they had done earlier in the century to labour in small workshops and in family businesses where only one or two men made the pieces and then passed on the craft skills to their sons, the German firms worked on a different basis (see page 66–7). If you look at a list of the recognized toymakers of the 19th century, you can see that of 47 listed in Britain in the mid-19th century, only seven survived to 1900; Germany had 52 manufacturers listed in the mid-19th century, of which 28 survived up until 1900. Of the 15 major American makers in the 19th century, nine started up between 1860 and 1880.

The German toymakers created everything for the dolls' house trade. There were specialists in tin kitchenware or stoves, in tiny ceramic teasets, metal goblets, copper kitchen utensils, metal bathroom fittings, prams, vases, bird cages and picture frames. Dolls might be of matt porcelain or bisque, glazed porcelain, wood and, later, celluloid. Others made dolls' houses. There were German blue roof houses, emulating slate, and red-roof houses, emulating tiles. Christian Hacker of

Nuremberg, working from 1875 until early this century, produced houses that look more French than German with mansard roofs, French windows and balconies.

One of the main inventions which the German manufacturers used to achieve lifelike but inexpensive houses was chromo-lithography. This had actually been invented in Germany at the end of the 18th century but the use of full colour was cracked after 1830. By printing with polished stone blocks, it was possible to create prints on paper with amazing detail and in full colour.

COLOUR PRINTING

Paper printed by chromolithography was used on both the dolls' houses and the furniture in them (see above right). The exterior features of brick and stone were printed and stuck on to a wood board, as were realistic door planks, ornate gilded handles and trellis work. A single house could have several varieties of brick (red and cream) marble, dressed stone and windows printed on to attic dormers – all of paper.

The same technique could produce realistic, if far too ornate, furniture. With printed paper the most complex patterns of marquetry and parquetry were possible, brass could be inlaid ad nauseam and the most costly and rare woods were available. It was, perhaps, lucky that over-ornamentation was in the highest fashion, for the toymakers seemed unable to restrain their wonder at the new technique. Often, indeed, the dolls' house furniture of this period would have been over the top even for a mid-19th century adult, but it was appealing to children. Birds cavort on drawer fronts, children gambol on table tops, every edge and knob is gilded.

In London, pewter was being used in increasing quantities. A journal in 1877 reported that "at one establishment one ton of metal is consumed each month in the production of Lilliputian tea, coffee and dinner sets". The metal came from recycled candlesticks, teapots and pans bought by the hundredweight, proving that recycling is not a new idea. "One girl can make 2,500 small tea-cups a day. Putting together the four separate pieces of gun metal, she fills it with the molten metal, dips its mouth into cold water, takes it to pieces and turns out a cup that only wants trimming."

In America, the makers were a bit more businesslike about the manufacturing process. Two important ones were George W. Brown & Co of Forestville, Connecticut, and J. and S. Stevens of Cromwell, Connecticut. Their catalogue included "all in the current adult styles" bureaux, wash stands, fruit baskets, stoves, coppers, coal hods and shovels, laundry tubs, sleds and sleighs, rocking and kitchen chairs, cradles, ottomans, mirrors, chopping bowls and dustpans.

△ A German set of drawing room furniture made with printed chromolithograph paper glued to wood. The pieces are very fancy, decorated with flowers, cupids and animals. The drawers of the chest open and the mirror is real. Note the deep fringe on the chair, typical of the 1880s.

▷ Dolls, like real people, enjoy garden pavilions for relaxation. This tiny gazebo opens out from a hexagonal box, complete with a set of sofa and two stools upholstered in purple velvet with a painted chest and round table. The top of the box is printed to look like a trellis and the walls like a flowery bower. The floor is tiled. It is German, from the 1870s, with chromolithograph printed paper on wood.

◁ This most unusual dolls' house from the 1870s sits on a neat set of drawers with carrying handles used to hold extra furniture and equipment. This is a carpenter-made house – a one-off – in this case made for a little girl by her grandfather, who was a cooper. It is English and made of wood with a classical front with plate-glass windows. On one side there is a smart conservatory and vinery, decorated inside with paper flowers.

▽ This extremely grand doll with her long train and spangled dress of lustrous cotton satin. She dates from the late 1870s and has a moulded ribbon in her moulded hair. She is German with bisque head and limbs.

DO-IT-YOURSELF

Although the era of home-made furniture and carpenter-made houses was coming to an end, it was very slow dying. Gordon house (above) was made as late as 1873 by an individual carpenter and has a delightfully eccentric conservatory – all the rage then as now – attached at one side as high as the third storey. Indeed, many women today still remember playing with a simple house made by their father, a friend, relative or the local handyman. In the late 19th century, those children not lucky enough to have a bought, German dolls' house would often have a home-made one, frequently constructed from hefty wooden storage boxes. These do-it-yourself dolls' houses often survive because of their hardiness.

Mrs Beeton herself gives handy advice on how to make dolls' furniture with black perforated cardboard and thin polished cane: "A curtain pole: push the ends of a bit of cane into two gilt beads. The sofa: the cardboard is of four thicknesses, and of oblong shape. It is then sewn with red filoselle in long stitches, both the length and breadth of the cardboard, forming a checked pattern. Now pierce holes through the four corners with a stiletto and take a long piece of cane, which must be pushed into the two holes at the back to form the frame. Two more holes are pierced in the back and through these another piece of cane is pushed and curved. It is fixed to the first piece by a small white stud in the middle. The second piece of cane furnishes the legs."

Mrs Beeton also gave advice on how make the house itself: "Endless as is the variety of amusements to be found for the little ones, nothing gives so much real and lasting satisfaction as a dolls' house and this, like many other things, can be made at home if there happen to be a good-natured big brother who will condescend to interest himself in the work. There are always packing cases about, stored away in cellar or attic, which could be spared for the purpose; this, then, with a few deal boards, some two-inch screws, a pair of hinges, some nails and smaller screws, a hasp for the door, glue-pot and, last, but not least, the willing brother or uncle with his box of carpenter's tools, can be quickly converted into a charming dolls' house."

She suggests using white foolscap paper pasted to the wood for ceilings and scraps of old wallpaper for the walls, "Only care must be taken that the pattern on the paper or papers is small, or the rooms will be dwarfed and ugly."

What her detailed descriptions show is the complexity of 19th-century family life when children had to provide their own amusements.

UNIQUE EXAMPLES

While Mrs Beeton was encouraging children to make their own dolls' house and furniture, there were still children fortunate enough to be given very smart hand-made dolls' houses. For instance, the dolls' house on the right was made in 1877 for 10-year-old Fanny Hayes, daughter of President Rutherford B. Hayes. It is one of two houses known to have graced the White House. The other dolls' house was also made for the privileged Fanny. Built a year later in 1878, it was a much grander affair – a handsome, ornate piece with a mansard roof, a grand portico and a spire, a piece of high Victoriana, rich in architectural detail. A woman journalist, allowed to visit the private quarters of the President and his family, spotted it: "Most agreeable reminders of the presence of children are the two large 'baby houses' standing in the hall, in which the President's only daughter, Fanny, between 10 and 11 years of age, and the youngest child, Scott, some three or four years younger, take great delight." The dolls' house had vanished into obscurity until the great-grandson of the President married a dolls' house enthusiast who lovingly restored it and replaced its vanished furniture. Even the maker's name turned up – George C. Brown, Baltimore, Md, with the date of 13th February, 1878.

△ This deep-buttoned daybed is part of a wonderful set of semi-professionally made furniture of the mid-19th century. It includes two armchairs, two pouffes and two footstools. The fabric has a tiny floral pattern and the hidden frames are of cardboard.

▽ Maddison Magruder made this dolls' house in 1877 for Fanny Hayes, the daughter of the president. The essential American style is now appearing, having cast off most European influences. Inside, there are six rooms and a staircase with a bannister.

A SILBER & FLEMING TOWNHOUSE

A town house, whether in London, Amsterdam or New York, is a boon to toymakers because nothing is simpler to construct than these tall terraced houses found in so many cities. This dolls' house is recognizably Georgian in style – but only just. The tall flat-fronted building has a stucco-covered ground floor, with ornamental bricks for the next two floors, and its scale of windows, small but grand on the ground, high and very grand on the first and slightly smaller on the third floor, follows the pattern of classical 18th-century buildings. So too, does the raised parapet which is intended to hide the roof and the metal balcony outside the three first floor windows. The front door, however, is unlike anything ever seen on a genuine Georgian terrace, although many 18th-century front doors are raised several steps above the pavement.

The windows of this type of terraced house were plate glass, which was introduced into houses from the 1850s onwards, taking the place of smaller panes and thin glazing bars. The window tax was also repealed in 1851 which meant that people felt happy to have as much light as they could. In this dolls' house, the windows of the two top storeys have green blinds painted on to the window glass; blinds were a feature of the mid-19th century.

This modestly priced plain little dolls' house, aimed at the British middle-class market, was produced for Silber & Fleming, the British firm of wholesalers. The firm was based in London and operated between 1850 and 1900 – quite a long time considering it was a period of great competition. They sold dolls' houses in a wide variety of sizes and styles, with a huge range of prices. This one is marked 7s 6d. It is made to

reflect the Victorian way of life, right down to the British bobby outside the front door. He is an all bisque doll with a bell-shaped helmet and black uniform decorated with little beads as buttons. The rooms are very basic, allowing children to change their uses as and when they wished. A nice touch in the kitchen is a home-made raffia basket for the two terriers.

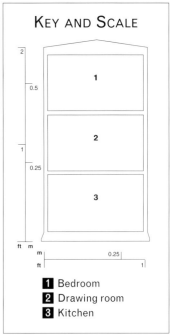

◁ The best Victorian town terraces were copied by Silber & Fleming. This London example has a lacy first-floor balcony and balustrade, blooming windowboxes and a gaudy front door.

DATE Made in Germany in the 1870s for the English wholesalers, Silber & Fleming.
SCALE 65cm (25in) high, 35cm (14in) wide and 22cm (9in) deep.
STRUCTURE The frame is made of wood in one piece with the single door hinged on the right and opening from the left. The wood is painted to simulate stucco on the ground floor, two-tone brick above (later versions used printed paper). There is a metal balcony which was a common feature of Silber & Fleming houses. The sides and back of the house have no architectural detail but are painted a dull red.
LAYOUT OF ROOMS Three simple rooms with no stairs. The wallpapers are cut-offs done for ordinary houses – no attempt was made to find small patterns.

KEY AND SCALE

1. Bedroom
2. Drawing room
3. Kitchen

◁ Silber & Fleming houses are very plain inside – here three rooms only. Architectural detail is minimal – fireplaces and chimneybreasts. They were known for using over-sized wallpaper, adaptable for many rooms.

◁ This is an elaborate and professionally made half-tester bed. From Germany, it has pea-green hangings – very fashionable – and a silk padded back. There is a lace-edged pillow. The bed's base is made from fine wire. It dates from the 1870s.

△ A fine blue glass has been moulded into little wine glasses, probably for German hock or champagne. They, and the heftier tumbler, are made in Germany.

▽▷ Two drawing-room pieces made in Germany around 1870. The table top is of chromolithographed paper with a pattern like Berlin woolwork but it was made specially to fit. The marquetry bookcase would originally have had glass doors which opened but are now missing. The turned pillars at the sides are of printed paper.

▽ The solidity and plainness of this little pine kitchen table means that is was probably made in England. It has tapering legs and two carved drawers. On top of the table there is a tiny set of white china with a blue pattern, made in Germany.

▷ A soft metal, elaborately moulded to simulate carving and turning, has been used for this rather grand child's high chair. The patterns are then bronzed. The "cane" of the chair seat is a fine pierced metal. The piece is German.

HOMES FOR CHARITY

In the United States the carpenter-made dolls' house tradition lingered, although energetic German makers were exporting even across the Atlantic. One notable example was exhibited at the Great Central Fair for the United States Sanitary Commission in Philadelphia, the oddly named body that raised funds for the sick and wounded soldiers who fought in the Civil War. It was valued at $1,000 and made by a Miss Biddle. An expert marble cutter had been hired to make its three tiny marble fireplaces (it took him three days) and the draperies were ostentatiously magnificent. The house even has an art gallery with works by Rubens and Salvator Rosa.

BACK TO BASICS

The *Daily Telegraph* of 1875 seemed to think building a dolls' house was quite easy – although it is unlikely the writer tried the feat himself: "A clever carpenter or joiner could put together a big dolls' house in a couple of days. It could be painted, glazed and dried in another twenty-four hours. Toy warehouses are full of all the miniature goods and chattels which would be required for the most luxurious dolls' house of the ordinary type. Admirably pretty upholstery, glass and china-ware, and drapery of this sort are made in England and France." Germany, even more so, he adds.

It is noticeable that Mrs Beeton considers the construction of the dolls' house male work – and the furnishings and interior for girls to make and to play with.

▽ An unusual English dolls' house dating from the 1880s, which hinges in the middle to reveal four rooms – perhaps for two children to play in. The house has been restored and the interiors are not contemporary. It is possible that it has been adapted from one of the designs illustrated for do-it-yourself makers who read woodworking magazines of the period.

She suggested that dolls with taste might like a dado on the walls of the reception room and offered the following advice to children: "If wanted very simple, turn out mother's collection of crests, pick out the darkest and arrange them as they look best…The crests should be stuck with gum as it is better for them than paste… A much more elaborate one can be made thus: collect all the old Valentines, Christmas cards etc. those you do not particularly care to keep, and pick off or cut out from them all the tiniest figures of birds, insects etc. These, with some bunches of flowers, miniature trees and tiny cupids disporting themselves in the shade will, if arranged so that the birds appear to be flying or perching on the branches of the trees and the insects crawling about beneath among the bright flowers and grasses make quite a charming dado." This, Mrs Beeton warns, although quite charming, is much more difficult to make.

MALE INTEREST

Although Mrs Beeton thought that dolls' houses were intended for girls to play with, there are a few exceptions. One house, Dingley Hall, in the Bethnal Green Museum of Childhood, London, was made in 1874 for two boys, Isaac and Laurence Currie. And very masculine it is. It seems that Laurence had taken an interest in and began collecting miniatures as a small child. Throughout his adult life he added to his collection. The house itself was named after a real house near Market Harborough, Leicestershire. It is very large with 13 rooms, starting with an entrance hall with a tiny, nude Greek goddess. The walls of the upstairs landing are decorated with shields, weapons, holding trophies, a stag's head and, rather incongruously, musical instruments. Most of the dolls who live at Dingley Hall are also male, whether footmen in uniform or military men, also in uniform.

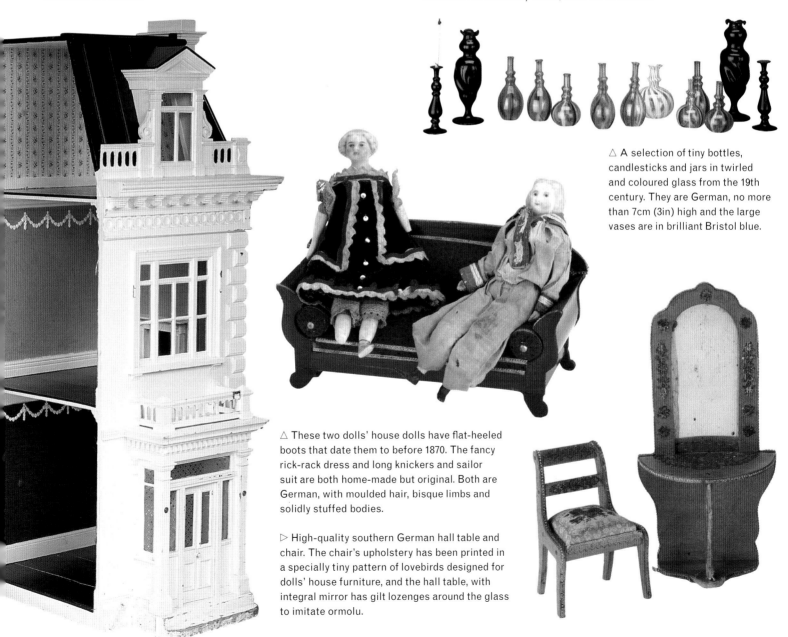

△ A selection of tiny bottles, candlesticks and jars in twirled and coloured glass from the 19th century. They are German, no more than 7cm (3in) high and the large vases are in brilliant Bristol blue.

△ These two dolls' house dolls have flat-heeled boots that date them to before 1870. The fancy rick-rack dress and long knickers and sailor suit are both home-made but original. Both are German, with moulded hair, bisque limbs and solidly stuffed bodies.

▷ High-quality southern German hall table and chair. The chair's upholstery has been printed in a specially tiny pattern of lovebirds designed for dolls' house furniture, and the hall table, with integral mirror has gilt lozenges around the glass to imitate ormolu.

German manufacturers cleverly designed their dolls' houses to suit other countries' architecture. The mansard roof and arched windows of Chateau St. Pierre, in Bordeaux, France (shown in the background) are reflected in this Christian Hacker dolls' house.

CHAPTER SIX

Fin-de-Siècle

1880–1914

As happens in the dying moments of a century, disillusion sets in and the 19th century was no exception. Victorian values were ridiculed, Victorian art was sneered at and Victorian architecture dismissed. Opulence was out, craftsmanship was in. Movements like the Arts and Crafts in Britain and *Jugendstil* in Austria dictated an end to clutter and a move to simplicity. But, as the mass-production of dolls' houses had overtaken all but the dedicated do-it-yourself enthusiasts, fashions in miniature began to lag behind. Dolls' house owners became less interested in smart decor and more in home values.

The period between 1880 and the start of the First World War in 1914 is the heyday of the dolls' house (although, curiously, the 1930s were another high-spot – the Depression or Slump causing parents to seek dolls' house security for their children where there was none in the real home). In Britain it seemed like a golden age: the country was prosperous and confident, with wars neatly taking place elsewhere. The horror of the First World War seemed a world away. Although wealthy, the developed world was nonetheless in *fin-de-siècle* mood, weary and cynical.

▽ Bel Air mansion was made by the American firm of Converse c.1885 and belonged to five sisters of the Dibb family. A special feature is the "captain's walk" where seamen's wives were supposed to pace, looking out to sea for their husband's return.

▷ Royalty and dolls' houses seem to have an affinity. The Duchess of Teck gave this modest six-room house to her daughter, Queen Mary, who collected numerous other houses. It was made c.1880 and is filled with both hand-made and commercial furniture.

The major reforms which made life civilized for the poor had been pushed through but children were still benefiting from the reformers' zeal. Socialism was in its infancy with the foundation of the Fabian Society in 1884 while, in 1891, free education was brought into Britain. The Boy Scouts, destined to become a worldwide movement, held their first camp in 1907. Children were now to be seen and heard, even if the emphasis was on boys (the Girl Guides were founded in 1910). This, too, was a period when earlier inventions were developed into practical machines. In 1884, Daimler invented the motor engine and by 1893, Henry Ford had produced his first car. On the heels of this, the London Underground was in use in 1890, the first movie was shown in 1895 and, in 1903, the Wright Brothers made their first flight. Cinemas had appeared by 1906. All these heralded the modern age of rapid communication between peoples and easier travel.

It was, too, the heyday of the dolls' house as a child's toy. The earlier Dutch cabinets and English baby houses may be more elegant, detailed and expensive but they were designed to indulge the fantasies of adults rather than as children's toys. By the late 19th century, many people in the civilized world could afford to buy their children toys (this was not the case even 40 years before). And the toys, thanks to by-products of inventions during the Industrial Revolution, were themselves less expensive and numerous.

△ Of unknown origin, this stately
dolls' house is in the Spanish
style. Its rooms are formal and
decorated with characteristic
heavy, over-patterned wallpapers.
The sweeping steps to the
entrance hall and the roof terraces
with their ornate balustrades are
also typically Mediterranean.

MAISON DE STYLE

French dolls' houses are quite rare. For some reason, the full-scale, many-roomed dolls' house is generally found in Northern Europe and America while Southern Europe seems to have preferred to make single-storey, open room settings. This *maison de style* (from the Musée des Art Decoratifs, Paris), however, is a genuine, carpenter-made dolls' house from France and, because of its detailed architectural personality, it may be a scaled-down version of a known house. It has been carefully made, probably as a one-off, and is very different from the commercially made dolls' houses of the period (see page 126). The styling of the arches in between the arched windows of the upper storey and the ashlar effect of the lower half of the house is most unusual, although the wide and grand double door is a common French feature, as are the beautifully made ornate iron grilles on the lower windows and the iron balustrades on the upper ones.

The base is unusual in having two diamond-shaped grilles under the windows. They may have been added to ventilate the dolls' house or to copy air and light grilles commonly found in basements of contemporary French houses. Although the style of the house is typically French, it contains an assortment of charming and eccentric pieces from Germany and France, many of which cannot be illustrated in detail because they are glued down. This – a conservator's nightmare – has had the benefit of keeping everything in its original place.

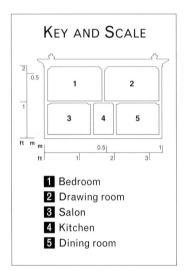

KEY AND SCALE

1 Bedroom
2 Drawing room
3 Salon
4 Kitchen
5 Dining room

◁ Like the dolls' house, this town house from Boulogne in northern France has an ashlar façade, a double door (albeit not quite as grand as the dolls' house) and iron balustrades on the arched windows. Although this particular house is not exactly the same as the dolls' house, it is apparent that the dolls' house was designed to mirror French architecture at the end of the 19th century.

▷ The whole façade lifts off to reveal the simple, five-roomed interior. Architectural detail inside the house is limited to cornices and fireplaces; the lovely furnishings enhance the décor. Electric light bulbs have been fitted in each room to illuminate the house.

DATE Made c.1885 (although some of the contents are earlier).
SCALE 62cm (24½in) high, 1m (39in) wide, 47cm (18½in) deep.
STRUCTURE The house is made from painted wood with windows at the side that have metal bars. The roof of faux slate is virtually hidden behind a heavy parapet. The façade lifts off to allow for play. (Now that the house is on display at the Musée des Art Decoratifs, a glass panel has been fitted to the front which allows viewing and prevents play.) The arched windows are glazed.
LAYOUT OF ROOMS The upper floor consists of a large drawing room and bedroom, while a salon, dining room and kitchen are found on the ground floor. The kitchen has been foreshortened more recently to accommodate batteries for the electric lights. There are no stairs or doors in the house.

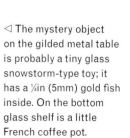

▷ Although it was made in Germany in about 1870, this rococo-style mirror looks very French. The soft metal has been gilded.

△ This triptych mirror closes up tightly and has landscapes painted on the two outer sides. It is German, of gilt metal and it dates from the 1870s.

◁ Made in Germany, this tiny oil lamp has a separate glass bowl and funnel but lacks a wick.

◁ This most charming French poodle is a miracle of tiny stitchery. The body is knitted silk with a bouclé stitch used to create the uncut front and pompom tail. The ears are kinked silk and the eyes are beads. It is very unusual and was more than likely made by a skilled seamstress specifically for the dolls' house.

▷ There are at least 12 tiny prints about 2.5cm (1in) wide hanging on various walls and showing children at play. They include a girl skipping, *la Corde,* and a boy with a parrot, *le Parroquet,* and must have been made especially for dolls' houses.

◁ The mystery object on the gilded metal table is probably a tiny glass snowstorm-type toy; it has a ¼in (5mm) gold fish inside. On the bottom glass shelf is a little French coffee pot.

THE RACE FOR REALISM

In the dolls' house world, mass-production was well established and makers were searching for new inventions that would make the houses cheaper (or more expensive), easier to carry, easier to create and more realistic. It seems that realism was the over-powering ambition for makers and buyers alike. Chromolithography was used to create complex patterns of decoration both for the house exteriors and the furniture inside; mass-production of pressed metals, from guns to weaving machines, could be adapted to create tiny, realistic pieces of furniture and new techniques in moulding and decorating china were used to make the dolls themselves.

A contemporary American account in *Harper's Young People* of an 1888 dolls' house and its young owner shows how far the industry had progressed in creating realism in miniature: "The dolls' house was very like what I remember in my own childhood – a three-storey dwelling with a very convenient front, for, by turning the knob of the front door, three storeys of window, entrance and all opened on hinges and disclosed the interior of doll's family residence. But how different it was from the doll house I cherished nearly 20 years ago (that is, in 1868)! We felt ourselves luxurious then with furniture selected from a large tray at our toy-shop for a penny each. But in my little friend's doll house I saw a drawing room which was an amusing imitation of the one in which I had just been having afternoon tea. The furniture was decorated with odd bits of drapery and the floors were painted and carpeted with a capital imitation of rugs. The mistress of this artistic dwelling was

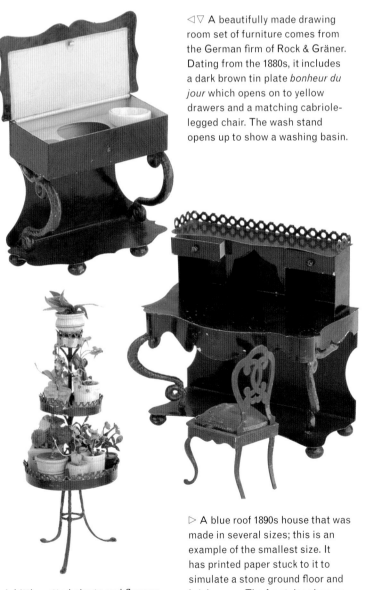

◁▽ A beautifully made drawing room set of furniture comes from the German firm of Rock & Gräner. Dating from the 1880s, it includes a dark brown tin plate *bonheur du jour* which opens on to yellow drawers and a matching cabriole-legged chair. The wash stand opens up to show a washing basin.

△ Little potted plants and flowers, made of cotton and glass, cover this very rare Rock & Gräner, three-tier plant stand.

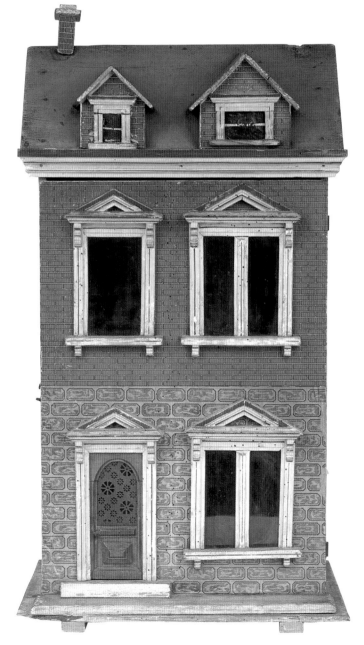

▷ A blue roof 1890s house that was made in several sizes; this is an example of the smallest size. It has printed paper stuck to it to simulate a stone ground floor and brick upper. The front door has an etched glass panel which indicates that this German toy may have been made for the English market.

seated in the drawing room near a low tea table and dressed in a most becoming tea gown."

Realism demanded that not only should objects look real but also that they should work. One early 20th-century collector of miniatures had no less than 28,000 objects(including an electric stove that baked a loaf and a working sewing machine) which he would take on tour in a single trunk.

Many of the dolls' houses themselves were replicas of the kind of buildings which were going up in their thousands on the edges of European cities. The real houses and the dolls' houses were simple and pleasantly proportioned, with neatly papered interiors, not unlike the house shown opposite and below. Not much later, however, the makers gave way to pressure from the children to veer to over-ornamented fantasies.

△▷ Whatever humans got up to, dolls also did. Here they play games of chess, draughts and dominoes on a rare German-made games table of about 1890. It is of simulated oak with the games top and cover of printed paper; little chessmen and other pieces are kept in the table well.

◁ The interior, of only two rooms, has its original wallpapers, both stripes and one with a leaf design. The windows have sills and catches to hold the curtains, which were generally of red or blue cotton but are missing. The large hanging lights of gilt metal have pink glass shades and were probably for gas. The painted soft metal furniture includes a magazine rack.

△ This German doll, with moulded hair, bisque limbs and a stuffed body, dates from around 1880. Her clothes, which show no sign of contemporary fashion, are home-made.

TECHNOLOGY TRIUMPHANT

In 1910, a dolls' palace was advertised for sale in America: "The entire front swings open and discloses to view five rooms… and an elevator, run by a clever mechanism, lighted by electricity running up through the cellar of the house and carrying dolls and doll necessities to the various chambers. Each room is fitted out with beautiful doll furniture." The same year, the English *Royal Magazine* noted a house where the fires would light and the smoke go up the chimneys. For every dolls' palace or mansion there were hundreds of commercially made dolls' houses like the examples shown here, some of which had the latest gimmicks and technology.

The first bathrooms appeared in dolls' houses in the mid-1880s. One of the earliest dolls' houses with an integral bathroom was found in San Francisco; it was made in 1886 and copies a row house in the city.

England, where, presumably, cleanliness was still next to godliness, was also making dolls' houses with real bathrooms

▽ Dating from 1910, this German tin-plate wash stand is painted to simulate woodgrain but has a real mirror and opens. The large washing set is made of cast metal and patterned in gold.

△ This is an all-bisque dolls' house doll with "sleeping eyes". She is German and was made c.1910. She has a large wig and typical bar shoes of the period.

◁ This small, but ornate, blue roof house of the 1890s is no more than 23cm (9in) high. It is German and made of printed paper glued to wood. All the detailing – side and front arched windows, brick and stone front, net curtains, blinds and climbing plants, are created in print.

where the dolls could take a bath. An American, seething at the $42 price for an English dolls' mansion reported "that a good business is to be done in these doll houses with bathrooms. One can get several different models. To play with water is the aim of many a little girl with good clothes to spoil." He goes on to explain how the feature worked: "These dolls' houses with baths generally have a fair-sized tank in the roof which, when filled, contains sufficient water to allow a whole doll family to be bathed. Some of the newer model doll houses have electric lights throughout, an installation costing $35. For $40, if the construction of your house will allow, you can have an electric elevator installed. This is electrically driven and the cost includes accumulator and motor."

This is all the more impressive when you realize that electric light was not used in real houses before 1881 and was not at all common until the late 1880s. Less than two decades later, inventors had solved the problems of reducing the whole system to fit a scale of 1:12.

It was not just the technologically advanced Americans who lusted after real equipment in their tiny homes. In 1907, *Royal Magazine* described a £25 dolls' house which was "a very desirable town residence, containing whole reception rooms, spacious bedrooms and

possessing many other attractions suitable for a nobleman, Member of Parliament or a gentleman." What did this grand gentleman doll need? "…pictures and mirrors on the walls, a billiard room, a motor garage, a lift to all floors, lock and key to the front door." The bath, naturally, filled with water which was heated by a little spirit lamp and the billiard table had balls to scale made of sugar. The male owner already had a car (22 years after its first invention).

◁ German makers created the most unlikely accessories for their houses using soft metal. On the left is a holder for bottles and glasses, with its original glass bottles and tumblers; on the right a sewing basket, lined with crepe paper. Both were made c.1900.

△ The German manufacturer Moritz Gottschalk was known for "red roof" houses (imitating tiles) and "blue roof" houses, (imitating slates), as illustrated here. The firm also occasionally equipped their ultra-modern houses with lifts. This blue roof dates from the late 19th century and is carefully detailed.

Whereas houses in the earlier years could be up to 274cm (9ft) high, the mass-produced dolls' houses of the late 19th century could be less than 23cm (9in) high, like the house shown left. This miniaturization was most appealing to children as well as being cheap to make. Machines meant that it was possible to create the decor details and furniture small enough to fit – pieces made by hand could never match the machine's ability to create in tiny scale. A child's love of over-the-top ornamentation – and children were by now having a say in their own toys – meant that the manufacturers created dolls' houses that could never have existed in real life.

KEY AND SCALE

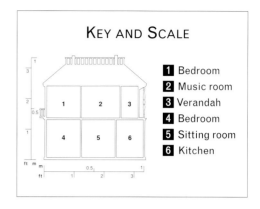

1 Bedroom
2 Music room
3 Verandah
4 Bedroom
5 Sitting room
6 Kitchen

DATE Made c.1880.
SCALE 107 cm (42¼in) high, 104cm (41in) wide and 41 cm (16in) deep.
STRUCTURE Made of wood over-papered with "brick" walls and "tiled" roof. It has no front but the back is carefully detailed with glazed windows and a stringing course between floors. One side is also given windows.
LAYOUT OF ROOMS There are six rooms with no staircase. The bottom floor has a bedroom, a sitting room for the lady of the house and a kitchen; above is another bedroom, a music room with prie dieu for devotions and an open verandah.

Although Germany provided toys for the world and produced styles characteristic of France, Britain and the United States, it is rarer to find commercially made dolls' houses that are typically German in feeling. This dolls' house is based on similar real houses which were built in Germany towards the end of the 19th century. The dormer windows in the roof and balustrade above can also be found both in 17th century real German houses and in carpenter-made dolls' houses of the same period. The open-air verandah on the first floor is another typically German feature. The house contains most of its original contents, including many religious icons, which suggests that it once belonged to a devout family.

△ In the 18th century, Germany admired and copied French achitecture. This country house is Château Mon Plaisir near Bayreuth. The symmetry, sharp roof with dormer windows and simple elegance of the house is reflected in the dolls' house.

◁ The Germans were early fanatics for healthy living and believed firmly in the advantages of fitness, exercise and fresh air. Houses, therefore, were designed with open-air rooms, larger than the average balcony, where refreshing draughts of air could be breathed. The whole family would meet here including the children.

A German Country House

◁ Toymakers were extremely ingenious in using all kinds of materials to achieve their effects. Here Rock & Gräner have taken and painted a plain porcelain top to incorporate into a trestle side wash stand. This is an extremely rare piece.

△ Hefty lidded beer steins, made of thick pottery with pewter lids, can be found in German and Dutch dolls' houses over a period of 300 years, as indeed they appeared in real life. One of these celebrates München beer.

▷ The American Isaac Merrit Singer invented the first sewing machine in 1852. Within years, dolls had them too. This version faithfully copies the large, trestle machine and comes with a pair of gigantic scissors.

▷ These extraordinary chandeliers of maidens and antlers hanging from the ceiling would have been found in real Bavarian castles, hunting lodges and large homes. Two of these unusual chandeliers turn up in the dolls' house. (There is also one in the German box room on page 132.)

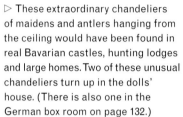

◁ Great care has been taken by the firm of Schneegas at Waltershausen to create a realistic white dial for this pendulum wall clock. The hands and figures of the porcelain face stand proud of the background for realism.

△ Meat covers like this miniature version became necessary once it was discovered how harmful flies are to health. Even dolls had to be protected against the germs they carry.

▽ Rock & Gräner had a liking for decoratively pierced metal and use it here as the base for a curly, three-wheel pushchair. In fact, it would have been highly uncomfortable, being both hard and draughty.

◁ Prussian officers enjoyed wearing their uniforms and this chap is in his full, military best with helmet, thigh-high leather boots and a sprinkling of medals. Full-dress German military figures, made and exported in quantity, turn up in unlikely places with admirals often being mistaken for butlers.

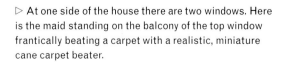

▷ At one side of the house there are two windows. Here is the maid standing on the balcony of the top window frantically beating a carpet with a realistic, miniature cane carpet beater.

SERVANTS WERE ESSENTIAL

A little girl, writing in 1891, stresses the importance of things working. Her new dolls' house had "real glass windows, a mantelpiece and doors that will open and shut. It has shades and curtains to the windows, a clock on the mantel and furniture. Afterwards my sister gave me a pug dog, a grey cat and a stove and coal scuttle and a doll named Dina to take care of the house. They are all the right size for the house and make it look real." Unwittingly, the little girl reveals the social custom whereby black dolls were automatically the servant class and generally seem to be called Dina or Dinah.

In France, where people were less concerned with owning an entire house of their own but just as concerned with keeping domestics in their place, makers produced a toy apartment block in 1911. It had six floors "of varying decoration, furniture and social status, each flat strangely complete from parlour to kitchen, all inhabited, with a doll janitor in his lodge by the great front door, two stairways and two elevators,

like the most expensive modern houses, the second elevator being a coal and provision lift for servants… there was electric lighting in each room of each apartment and complete electric heating."

Servants constantly appear in dolls' houses from those in the early 16th-century houses to the little tweenies, as they were known, with bobbed hair and uniform snoods that still turn up in the 1920s. The French chef is generally a magnificent figure, as is the cook and butler; others, like the French servants, are expected to keep out of sight in special lifts and their premises in attics or basements. At this time, dolls' houses might have servants' rooms (decorated with cast-off furniture) but earlier ones lacked any dormitories. But, then, so did the real houses – living-in servants might simply sleep under the kitchen table or on the lower shelf of the dresser.

Most middle-class people did, of course, have living-in servants until the Second World War and it is therefore perfectly correct that they should be included in dolls' houses.

◁ ◁ The lithographed paper on wood house far left is based on the sort of house found in the French seaside resort of Deauville. Both of these houses were probably made in Germany and the bases appear to be covered with the same rough ground effect. However, each has an individual style, illustrating what a very different effect printing can give.

◁ This house (left) is also influenced by the popular seaside resorts of Northern France. It has much more quirky detail than the house next to it. The stubby tower can be seen in reality in Northern France and the curious panels on the walls also appear in real life – although not vertically as here. It was made in the early 20th century.

▷ Another version of the Gottschalk house shown on page 117 with several openings which allow three or more children to play at once. This is a less expensive version but has the characteristic base covered with brick-printed paper. It was probably intended for the English market, since American Gottschalk houses have not been found with this detail.

Is there, too, some element of wishful thinking in that children without real servants to pick up their discarded clothes and toys could staff their dolls' houses with maids and cooks and therefore advance themselves socially? No doubt some mothers would go along with this, hoping the little girls would learn how to control staff in the event of an advantageous marriage. To be fair, other dolls' houses were made with the prosaic intention of teaching little girls the fun of housework; one American version was made with an open side so the child could "get inside to sweep and dust" – as though such tasks did not arrive of their own accord all too soon.

FRENCH ARCHITECTURAL STYLE

French dolls' house manufacturers were worrying about getting the style exactly right, for France was the leader of the world in elegance. At the Paris Exposition of 1900, a writer reported on a house where the "architecture was important,

with turrets, a bell-tower, banisters, flights of steps, balconies and encorbelments; dolls were at the windows watching a croquet match briskly played by their little sisters in the court-yard fenced with beautiful iron grill-work."

France, however, has little tradition in making dolls' houses, though they excel in creating larger scale dolls for children. Nearly all the impetus came from Northern Europe, most especially Germany. By the time little French children caught on to the idea, Germany had cornered the toy trade so only a few, carpenter-made French houses are now in existence. German makers like Gottschalk and Christian Hacker were astute enough, however, to make dolls' houses especially for the countries to which they exported. Thus there are German English bobbies, German houses for French seaside resorts and German houses for French bourgeois dolls.

△ Mansard roofs, invented by the French architect François Mansart in the 17th century, remained popular in France for centuries. This is a 19th-century house in Northern France, with similar features copied in the dolls' house.

DATE Made 1895–1900.
SCALE 71cm (28in) high, 68cm (27in) wide and 39cm (15½in) deep.
CONSTRUCTION Printed paper on a wooden carcase. The house comes apart in slices – the roof lifts off to reveal the attic which in turn lifts off. Each of the two main storeys also comes apart. The front of each main storey swings open to reveal the rooms.
LAYOUT OF ROOMS The ground floor has a dining room and kitchen. Stairs lead from the entrance hall to the first floor. The first floor has a living room and bedroom and there are two attic rooms.

A CHRISTIAN HACKER DOLLS' HOUSE

Christian Hacker, the German dolls' house manufacturer (founded in 1870), specialized in pretty French-style houses with typical mansard roofs and diamond roof tiles – the sort of house you see in northern provincial French towns.

The houses were exported all over Europe and the United States. They were extremely popular and were produced in a variety of designs and sizes. Each house is marked with an intertwined CH topped by a little crown. Hacker also made copies of English houses using, apparently, real examples in Balham and Clapham, South London. However, these have not yet come to light.

This particular house was made quite late in Christian Hacker's production, probably around the turn of the century. It is a cheaper version than the earlier houses and uses brick-printed paper rather than paint (see pages 7 and 109). The roof is simulated blue slate, which is very typical of Hacker houses, with a darker line around the edge, another distinguishing point. The detailing is still good, with each stone of the carved groins being outlined with blue. The balcony and balustrades which were also typical are missing from this house but it still has its doorbell, which actually rings.

▽ Once the roof is removed the two-roomed attic is revealed. It has a door joining the two rooms and, like the rest of the house, its original wallpaper. In the late 19th century attics would have been used for the servants' quarters.

KEY AND SCALE

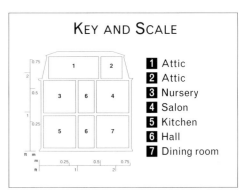

1 Attic
2 Attic
3 Nursery
4 Salon
5 Kitchen
6 Hall
7 Dining room

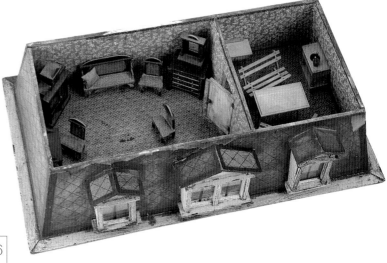

◁ The rather crude dressing table with no drawers, only a single cupboard, would have had a piece of real mirror glass fitted above but this has been replaced with silver paper. It is German and made of heat-embossed softwood.

▷ A corner cupboard from the drawing room is elegantly painted with a shepherd boy and girl plus pet lamb. It is one of a set of eleven drawing room pieces, including chairs, tables and a sofa, made in Germany. The patterns are created with chromolithographed scraps and gold paper bands.

△ This rocking cradle is made of tinplate and holds an early Celluloid baby doll. The doll has been ingeniously constructed with hidden lead weights so that it waves its arms and legs about as the cradle rocks.

▷ In common with German houses made over 200 years before, this house has, tiny sets of food. There is a leg of lamb on a cardboard plate, a colourful bowl of fruit (probably made by Bestikon, London) and a cake on a china plate.

△ In the 19th century, dolls' houses showed life among the bourgeoisie as well as the great. This is a simple interior with simple furnishings, although the upstairs salon shows the bourgeois "best room" at its most unfriendly.

△ The helmet pattern copper coal scuttle is probably much earlier in make – and certainly in style – than the house. It is beautifully made with a great eye for detail – note the two carefully shaped handles and scuttle lip.

MASS-PRODUCTION

In the period between 1880 and 1914, the Germans still dominated the world toy market. In the United States, for instance, 25 percent of toys were made in the country and 75 percent of toys imported, mostly from Germany. In 1894 the New York *Daily Tribune* was writing that most dolls' houses "come from Germany in the style of the modern suburban villa with real windows and having carpets on the floor". This domination was brought to an abrupt halt in 1914 by the outbreak of the First World War and by 1918 the United States made 90 percent of its own toys.

One of the most famous American toymakers was the Rufus Bliss Manufacturing Company founded in 1832 in Pawtucket, Rhode Island. But it was not until 1889 that the firm introduced the range of papered wood houses that are universally known as Bliss houses. The first version was immodestly described as "the best 50 cent house on the market".

Colour lithographed paper was used on the main range of Bliss houses, which appeared to universal acclaim in 1895. The houses were brilliantly coloured, small-scale and full of intricate detail which this printing technique allowed – even encouraged. That Bliss were proud of their range is obvious: the name R. Bliss is printed on doors, under gables and hidden on floors. This careful branding has added to the fame of Bliss, since almost every Bliss house can be identified.

Although Bliss houses differ widely, there are also similarities in design. They are very clearly American houses, with

△ This is an elaborate Bliss house that bears a strong resemblance to the house in Hitchcock's thriller *Psycho*. At the turn of the century, Bliss houses represented the height of middle-class desirability, with an attached turret, verandah, and fancy curtains at the windows.

▷ Bliss had the idea of teaching the alphabet by adding it to dolls' house furniture. As a result, these chromolithographed drawing room furnishings are known as ABC sets. They date from around 1901 and include an upright piano and stool, sofa, chairs and small games table. It would appear that ABC furniture was not intended to fit into Bliss dolls' houses, which were small in scale compared with the furniture.

△ A simple and inexpensive house by Rufus Bliss from the main 1895 range. Its wooden structure is covered throughout with carefully printed paper designs including windows. Chromolithography, a recent invention, meant that paper could be colour printed with an extraordinary range of imitation wood graining, brick, stone, tile and slate and then simply glued to the wooden frame.

▷ Bliss houses took architectural ideas from all over the world. This bright example seems to have a gipsy caravan-shaped first floor balcony with a net-curtained window behind. Below is a traditional American covered verandah with the turned wood balusters that are a regular Bliss feature. The printed faux rosewood front door is a triumph of excess with heavy panels and a net- and blind-covered central window.

verandahs, porches, balconies, cupolas and balustrades everywhere. While the styling is wildly eclectic, taking ideas from German gingerbread houses and from Californian beach houses, at the same time Bliss houses reflect American late-Victorian architecture.

Constance Eileen King comments that dolls' house makers of this period made claims about the educational and artistic value of their toys, feeling that pure enjoyment was not very noble. And Bliss's assertions that these houses are "true to nature in all respects" and "designed and modelled by a practical architect" are rather exaggerated. They were, however, suited to small modern houses and ideal for children, being inexpensive with a great deal of detail. Just the sort of house a little girl would dream of owning when she grew up.

The Bliss style was imitated in Europe and by rival American manufacturers such as Converse and Schoenhut. The firm of Bliss also created shops, stables, churches and other buildings, as well as dolls' house furniture.

△ Someone has cleverly adapted a set of bookshelves to make a very smart house of about 1900. The dolls are known as "people dolls" with bisque busts, arms and legs and lots of character. The house is probably Scandinavian with German dolls.

△ A cupboard house with seven fully-stocked rooms (c.1900). Although made in Germany, its cool decor looks destined for the Swedish market. The chef is in his grand basement kitchen with the servants' hall adjoining. There is also a standard lamp, so electricity must have arrived.

By 1889, Britain decided to get into the act with the foundation of the English Toy Company. "The toy that the company particularly prides itself upon bears the attractive name of Miss Dollie Daisie Dimple. This young lady is provided with an elegant detached villa, tastefully furnished, and with all kinds of necessaries and luxuries. She has also a travelling trunk, which contains no less than fifty-four articles, including several fashionable frocks and hats…" – a Victorian Barbie no less.

She lived in "an elegant detached villa of imitation red brick and stone facings, bay windows, green venetian blinds, bright colours…The interior decorations are all in the modern style. Dados, Bright Wallpapers etc. Can be taken to pieces and packed flat for transit or storage and can be rebuilt in seconds… It is quite a large Doll's House and takes the place

of a Doll's House usually costing ten times the money. Price ONE SHILLING complete." The young girls who were employed to make Dollie Daisy had less exciting lives. "The youngsters in their cottage homes find very congenial employment in… building up dolls' houses and the English Toy Company certainly does them a good service in enabling them to earn a few shillings weekly and at the same time, keeping them out of mischief."

NATIONAL DIFFERENCES

Dolls' houses were now being made all over the developed world. There is a carpenter-made Finnish dolls' house, dated 1890, in the Museovirasto in Helsinki. It is notable for four very high rooms with the tiny furniture all crowded at the bottom.

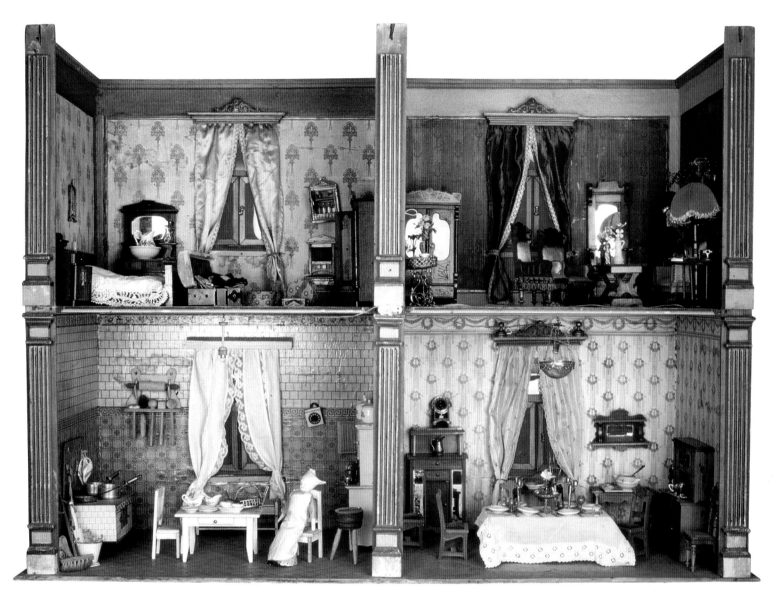

△ These German "open rooms" of c.1909 had a Danish owner, probably Benedigte Boldbrohoj of Ringsted, near Copenhagen, whose name is pencilled on the back. All rooms have original décor, and objects include a doll's trunk, hatboxes, medicine cabinet and plaster food.

The style is northern gloomy – dark wallpapers, heavy sideboards and, in the dining room, two graphic pictures of dead game birds hanging from hooks.

The Villa Olga, made by a Copenhagen furniture maker for 11-year-old Olga, is equally northern but more cheerful. Each floor is painted a different, bright, colour – scarlet, Scandinavian blue, white tiles in the kitchen – and each room, including the kitchen, is curtained with white, filmy curtains. This was a typical carpenter-made dolls' house as were those played with by Russian children. One refugee of the Russian Revolution remembers her mother painting a real oil painting copied from a seascape by the artist Aivazovski. The little girl turned her kaleidoscope into "a telescope in my doll house for my learned dolls who studied astonomomy and watching the comet of 1911". It is interesting how dolls of different nationalities reflect the character of the people.

A Scottish house of the period, for instance, has luggage, golf clubs and big-game rifles, the Scots being known explorers and upholders of the British Empire, while in the Empire itself Victorian values continued unabated. A New Zealand dolls' house, with Miss Queenie Watson inscribed on a brass plate on the front door, belonged to two little girls in Dunedin. One was tracked down by the people who had bought her house and revealed that "her parents only allowed them to view it only so often, and they were never allowed to play with it or ever to touch it". It was, of course, in good condition.

More tragic still was the treatment of Margaret Strong, owner of a dolls' house that was a replica of James Russell Lowell's house in Cambridge, Massachusetts. It was bought in a Red Cross benefit and was completely furnished. When she was eight, her parents started to travel and she would take a small bag filled with favourite dolls and toys that became her

friends and comfort. But every year, just before Christmas, her parents insisted she gave away her "most cherished toy", in theory to make room for presents to come. "I kept the dolls' house because I never admitted it was my treasure until I was 12 years old, when I gave it to my cousins." They managed to lose all its furniture and turned it into a storage cupboard, but she later retrieved it for her six-year-old daughter. Not surprisingly, she later became an avid dolls' house collector.

HOUSES IN KITS
Although there were plenty of dolls' houses in the shops by now, people were still making more characterful ones themselves (or employing professional cabinet makers and carpenters to do the work to their design).

Ingenuity was shown by an American journalist, Gertrude Okie Gaskill, who described in 1901 *How I Made a Dolls' House*. Old glass negatives were cleaned and cut to make windows, the face of a toy watch became a grandfather clock, and a school slate became a hearth. She also created a fur rug from a chipmunk which had been shot as bait for a sparrowhawk. She cured it but, unfortunately, the head "had been cut off, else the rug would have been in every particular like a large one".

△ Real French dolls' houses, as opposed to German ones in the French style, are rare. This one is made of printed cardboard and opens in the centre via a typical double door. The mansard roof, balcony and ornate window surrounds are found everywhere in French late 19th-century buildings.

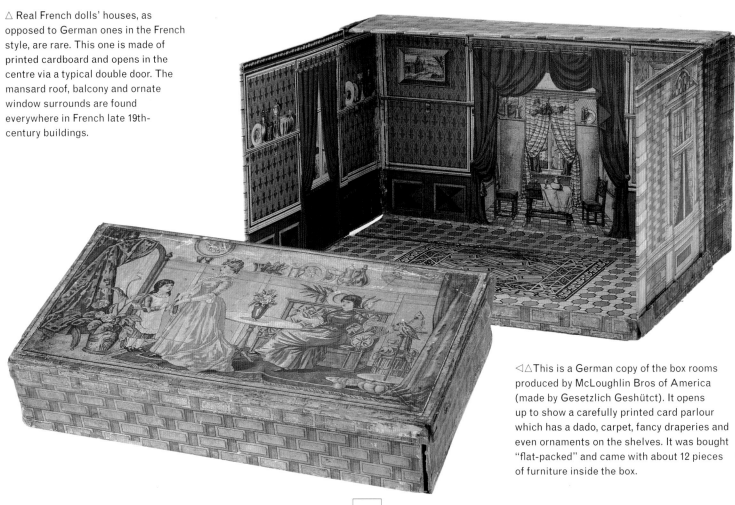

◁△This is a German copy of the box rooms produced by McLoughlin Bros of America (made by Gesetzlich Geschütct). It opens up to show a carefully printed card parlour which has a dado, carpet, fancy draperies and even ornaments on the shelves. It was bought "flat-packed" and came with about 12 pieces of furniture inside the box.

A halfway house was to buy a kit or construct your own with helpful instructions. One, "The House that Daddy Built" cost only two or three dollars compared to $35 for the bought article. The four-room house had its own little pulley lift and four tiny electric lights. The front door was "up-to-date oak with a little diamond window" and there was "a cosy verandah". Another house, described in 1914, listed 15 essential pieces of furniture the smart dolls' house must possess – library table, William Morris chair, writing desk, grandfather clock, dining table and chairs, buffet, reading lamp, bedstead, wardrobe, wash stand, ice-box, kitchen table, stove and cabinet.

As always, the kit houses, advertised as "simply assembled" turned out to be nightmares of confusion. Flora Gill Jacobs takes a sentence from one, an English kit of 1883, to describe the whole: "As the boxes are drawn apart, and turn on the hinges, the point A travels along the dotted circle, in the direction of the arrow, to A', F to F', C to C' and D to D',the points B and E describing semicircles, which it is unnecessary, on account of the space that would be taken up, to show in the diagram." Unsuspecting parents giving such kits at Christmas must have spent a nightmare day of oaths, tears and cut and glued fingers. As a result, many parents paid out the few extra dollars, shillings or francs and bought one ready-made.

Other kits were made of printed cardboard that came to pieces or folded, and these had the advantage of being able to be packed for travel. McLoughlin Bros of New York was the best-known manufacturer. In their catalogue (c.1876) they listed a dolls' house that consisted of two simple pieces of straw board which were slotted together on to a base to make a four-room apartment. The catalogue explained that the house was "designed to be played with on a table. A number of little girls may thus get around it to the very best advantage." The house included a parlour, dining room, bedroom and kitchen. McLoughlin used printed paper to create detailed interiors complete with potted palms, stags' heads and fires either blazing or covered with mimsy fans of paper (see page 8). The rooms reflect the middle-class American ideal lifestyle.

Miss Dollie Daisy Dimple's Villa made by the English Toy Company c.1889 (see page 130), also packed flat for storage and took only a few minutes to set up.

▽ An elaborate, although inexpensive, dolls' house made of printed cardboard. It dates from c.1910 but its asymmetrical arrangement of windows and the long hall and staircase window are clearly influenced by the *fin-de-siècle* designs of Charles Rennie Mackintosh and the Arts and Crafts movement. The front door at the side, set in its own bay, is a common feature of the time.

A G.&J. LINES DOLLS' HOUSE

Towards the end of the 19th century, G.&J. Lines were the most important toymakers in Britain. The London brothers, George and Joseph, started to produce such toys as rocking horses and prams in about 1858 and, by 1877, Joseph Lines was describing himself as a toy-maker. He was the businessman of the partnership and his brother George, the artistic one, was quickly bought out by Joseph.

Joseph put his four sons, William, Walter, George and Arthur, to work in the business. As soon as they left school, they were employed doing some of the nastiest work in the factory (cleaning cows' tails to make into horses manes, for example). By 1895, the firm had expanded to several factories in London and made, as well as horses, carts and prams, a huge variety of dolls' houses. These cost from 1s 3d up to a stupendous 65s; any over 8s 6d had curtains. They were built to last, even with constant play – and last they did, since so many survive to this day. Joseph did little to change the styles of his houses once they were popular, as can be seen from the 1910 catalogue which still featured many designs over 15 years old.

G.&J. Lines offered an excellent service, extending to repairing the houses. They also boasted "The papers used… have been specially printed and are delightful miniatures of some beautiful designs used by high-class decorators. The… woodwork is, in all cases, beautifully white enamelled and gold lined. The construction of our model houses is, above all, strong and artistic. Designs call forth praise from all who see them." Joseph Lines knew all about marketing.

▷ Spacious and well-designed, this double-fronted detached London house c.1885 has the same heavy treatment of windows and doors as the dolls' house. The enormous bay windows gave room interiors extra light.

DATE Made c.1900.
SCALE 84cm (33in) high, 69cm (27in) wide and 38cm (15in) deep.
CONSTRUCTION Made of wood, the house has been covered with paper printed with bricks. Imitation stucco surrounds, made of wood, have been applied around the arched windows. Gold

highlights have been added to the windows and the balusters on the roof. The house opens on two sides, each with access to two rooms.
LAYOUT OF ROOMS There are four rooms, all with original wallpaper. On the right-hand side is a dining room and bedroom; on the left-hand side, a kitchen and bedroom.

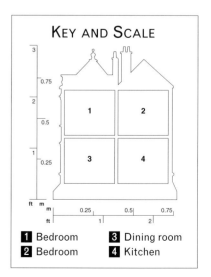

KEY AND SCALE

1	2
3	4

1 Bedroom   **3** Dining room
2 Bedroom   **4** Kitchen

▷ Old habits die hard. This enamelled tin ewer and basin set would be pretty much out of date by the early 20th century when most houses had running water. Nevertheless, this Art Nouveau-style German toy was still found in dolls' houses.

▷ This tin basket is actually a "penny toy" to tempt children with pocket money and made in Germany around 1900. These pieces are highly collectable in their own right. The tin is enamelled and the lids have a tight spring.

◁ This German dresser has been taken from the kitchen of the house. The ornamental design is printed onto the wood and a strip of fancy paper has been glued to the inside. It dates from about 1890.

◁ A chair from Germany is 1860 in style and is part of a bedroom set. Green fabric is set into the back. Beside it is a soft-metal sewing basket of faux bamboo. It is also German and, when you lift the lid, inside there are little reels of cotton.

▽ This Lines house opens on both sides and each side has two rooms. A clever idea that allows two children to play with the same house at one time. The wallpaper of this house is original. The fireplace is tinplate with, above it, a deer's head.

Flat-roofed and balconied
suntrap houses were better-
suited to the South of France.
However, this 1930s dolls' house
version (made by Tri-ang)
caught on in rainy England.
In the background is Landfall
House, overlooking Poole
Harbour in Dorset – a fine
example of Modernism
designed by the famous English
architect, Oliver Hill in 1938.

CHAPTER SEVEN

The Modern Era

1914 onwards

The split between the fashionable architecture of Le Corbusier and the Bauhaus and the actual status symbols of the rich was complete. Most wealthy families did not want "machines for living in"; they preferred Tudorbethan mansions surrounded by manicured gardens – houses with beams and inglenooks like the original but without the discomforts. Little girls wanted the status symbols too. Enough Stockbroker Tudor dolls' houses were made to build whole garden suburbs and enough vacuum cleaners, radiograms and refrigerators were made to fill them.

Modern dolls' houses (those made after the First World War to the present day) are not pieces of history, mysterious glimpses of the past that show us how life was lived long ago; instead they show us life as it was lived within human memory. If we cannot ourselves speak from experience of the 1920s and 1930s we have probably known people who could. We may have family snapshots and photographs, pieces of furniture owned by our grandparents, and vague memories of ancient gas cookers and electric fires. When we look at 20th-century dolls' houses, we are at last able to see how closely these miniature worlds do reflect real life and encapsulate those features we most remember of a given period. In the 20th century we also see the continued fascination of dolls' houses as both a child's toy and an adult's preoccupation.

Children with a new dolls' house are indulging in a fantasy that is shared by their parents. The family may be living in a council flat, or a wartime prefab or a condemned tenement in the inner city, but they can dream. And what they dream of is the current fashion of the period. They dream of a thatched cottage with roses round the door, or a Tudor house with parquet floors and a tennis court; they dream of kitchens stocked with the latest equipment – a refrigerator, a vacuum cleaner, a toaster – and dining rooms furnished with the latest neo-Georgian set of chairs. And this is what the dolls' house has provided. The dolls' houses from the first half of the 20th century remind us of dreams gone by, of the days we longed for a radiogram or a retreat in the country.

MODERNIST VERSUS POPULAR TASTE

Dolls' houses, too, are accurate guides of popular taste. At the end of the First World War, it was, generally, the most shattered nations that started the move towards modernism. After

▽ The Michelham Priory dolls' house of East Sussex was made in the 1920s and evokes many aspects of the period. The nursery has a cartoon border, tweenies cook in the kitchen and lay the heavy oak table, and the living room is comfortably busy. Bathrooms, however, are still bleak and clinical in feel.

the German defeat, the Bauhaus style, which looked to industry for its inspiration, appeared in 1919; Russia quickly turned to Constructivism in 1917 after the October Revolution that toppled the Tsars and introduced Communism; while neutral Holland, the same year, produced the art group De Stijl. The work of Walter Gropius and Ludwig Mies van der Rohe, of Gerrit Rietveld and Piet Mondrian, and of Vladimir Tatlin is still revered by modernists today. Their furniture, especially chairs, are still to be found in the most modern homes. But these designers were never taken to the hearts of the mass of the population, who remained unimpressed by their strange shapes, use of tubular steel and industrial processes. In Britain, we dreamt of Devon cottages; in Germany of Black Forest homes with rural shutters and views of the mountains; and in the United States of old-fashioned New England clapboard houses. And it is these houses that are copied for dolls.

The United States, still unsure of its own taste and having been isolated from Europe for the six years of the war, still believed France to be the world arbiter of taste and, in the mid-1920s, displays of French furniture toured the major New York stores of Saks, Macy's and Lord & Taylor. However, the United States also had its avant-garde and one of the most interesting dolls' houses of the early 20th century was created in the 1920s by New Yorker Carrie Stettheimer in the old carpenter one-off tradition (see above). The family was

highly sophisticated and artistic and knew the avant-garde artists of the day. Carrie was the dolls' house enthusiast, her sister Florine was a painter and her sister Ettie a poet. The dolls' house, in its modernism and adult sophistication, more nearly recalls the early Dutch and German cabinet houses – it was not a plaything but a miniature version of a smart house with all the latest designs and gadgets.

The Stettheimer dolls' house is in the Cubist-Corbusier modernist style (although the chef still rules over a large kitchen). It is especially interesting because Carrie included all the newest conveniences found in a New York house: there is a lift; the bathroom has a set of scales (the short flapper dresses of the period meant that you had to be slim); there is a wooden icebox waiting for deliveries from the iceman (you put a message in the window asking for so many chunks); and there is an outdoor terrace decorated with two modern sculptures after Epstein. There is more art in the ballroom – this is a dolls' house for a doll who entertains a great deal – but it is extremely modern. There are paintings by Archipenko, Albert and Juliet Gleizes and Carl Sprinchorn as well as the most famous of all,

◁ This, claimed the makers, Lines Brothers, is an exact reproduction of a dolls' house made famous by Queen Mary. She furnished the first model made (c.1922) and gave it to a London Hospital in order to raise funds.

a miniature version of Marcel Duchamp's *Nude Descending a Stair*. The house also has its own dolls, mostly in black tie and cocktail dresses, and very chic they are too.

The avant-garde Stettheimer house is a one-off modernist example, however, other areas of modernist interest did enthuse the public and did appear in many 20th-century dolls' houses. In 1913, in an America hardly touched by the war

except for its isolation from Europe, Christine Frederick wrote *The New Housekeeping*, which advocated a new type of kitchen. Since servants were becoming an endangered species, she suggested that kitchens should be as small as possible, intended simply for cooking (laundry and eating to be done elsewhere), and that they should be ergonomically thought out. While it was fine for the servants to walk miles a day between hob and worktop, it was not right for the mistress to do so. This was the birth of the modern kitchen.

One of the first important domestic changes after the First World War was in the kitchen. Christine Frederick's book did not arrive in Berlin until 1922. A year later, Marcel Breuer designed a fitted kitchen for the first Bauhaus exhibition. It had overhead storage units, a continuous work top and a row of storage jars above the units. Apart from its aged-looking water heating device, it could be a kitchen in any 1950s house. Three years after that, in 1926, Walter Gropius produced another fitted kitchen for the Bauhaus director's house with a rack of hanging implements, fitted storage units and an eye-level oven; the same year the designer Grete Schutte-Likotzky invented a foldaway ironing board.

△ Y Bwthyn Bach was originally built in 1932 by the Principality of Wales as a child-size play house for young Princess Elizabeth. It was copied by Tri-ang in Britain in several versions – some opening at the front, such as this, others from the back (see right). All, however, played on the fantasy of a little Welsh thatched cottage.

▷ The interior of another Y Bwthyn Bach dolls' house made by Tri-ang. The drawing room has a decorated Christmas tree and Santa Claus. The bedroom includes a tiled fireplace and fantasy four-poster bed (made at Westacre, Norfolk). The bathroom even has its own roll of lavatory paper.

Although these carefully organized workspaces, which treated the business of cooking with the same thoroughness as a factory production line, did eventually catch people's imagination, other modernist beliefs were ignored. People were not interested in Le Corbusier's famous remark that a house was "a machine for living in", they did not take kindly to reinforced concrete as a building material and they did not, like the Bauhaus pioneers, dismiss all ornament as degenerate. Rather, even in real life, they escaped to a fantasy land of rural bliss.

FANTASY WORLDS

While Modernism was the creed of the avant-garde, the public in Britain was creating a riot of Stockbroker Tudor and thatched cottages, and the slightly more design conscious were looking towards an updated version of William Morris, and the Arts and Crafts Movement of the Cotswold School, or of Gordon Russell. France, or more particularly Paris, was indulging in its own lush style of Art Deco, introduced by an exhibition in 1925. Jacques-Emile Ruhlmann of the shark-skin and shagreen cocktail cabinet was its most famous proponent. Scandinavia adopted Modernism more thoroughly – but a home-produced version that reflected its traditions of warm soft interiors created in light, soft woods such as pine and birch.

△ Mock Tudor was all the rage during the 1930s, perhaps as a nostalgic barrier against the Depression. This house (c.1936) is known as the Dolly Varden house (part of the Dinky Toy range for girls). It is made of printed cardboard that is decorated with climbing plants and pretty unrealistic oak beams. Originally it would have had a large garden.

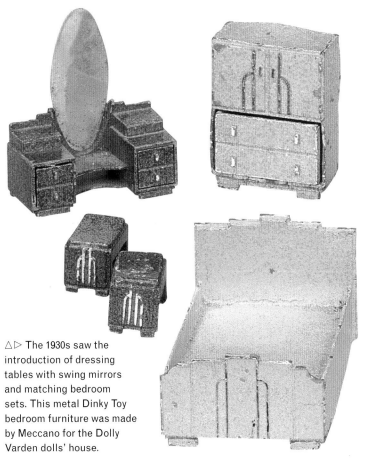

△▷ The 1930s saw the introduction of dressing tables with swing mirrors and matching bedroom sets. This metal Dinky Toy bedroom furniture was made by Meccano for the Dolly Varden dolls' house.

A GOTTSCHALK MODERNIST HOUSE

The architectural constants of Modernist houses are a flat roof (unhelpful in Northern Europe which has a high rainfall), the use of metal-framed windows and walls of painted stucco. Modernist buildings are rare, while even the toned-down houses that were built during the 1930s failed to dislodge the classic semi-detached house found in every suburb in Britain and similar houses in other countries.

△ An example of Bauhaus-style housing at Silver End in Essex. Most Modern Movement houses both in Britain and the United States tended to be individual architect-designed houses. Silver End is of one of the few housing developments built in the Modernist style.

▷ The view from the open back of the dolls' house shows all six rooms decorated and furnished in contemporary 1930s style with many of the latest gadgets. The wallpapers are all original – the kitchen and the bathroom both have a typical half-tiled look.

It was the same with Modernist dolls' houses. They are rare because they were not particularly popular at the time. Now, however, they are of immense interest to the collector. The Modernist dolls' house featured here was made in Germany by Moritz Gottschalk (c.1935) in the Bauhaus style. The English firm of Lines Bros (later known as Tri-ang) also made an ultra-modern dolls' house (see pages 136–7). However, their Stockbroker Tudor dolls' house (see pages 148–9) was far more popular at the time and is easily found today, as is the furniture that was made for it.

Gottschalk and Lines Bros both made dolls' house furniture, but specialist makers, such as the British firms of Taylor & Barnett and Dinky Toy, as well as several unrecorded German companies, were the only producers of Modernist furniture during the 1930s. They produced tubular steel chairs (including the architect Marcel Breuer's Wassily chair) and furniture such as day beds with a distinct Cubist influence. However, although such pieces are generally sought out by collectors today, they do not generally reflect the design ideas of 1930s children.

DATE Made c.1935.

SCALE 50cm (20in) high, 75cm (29in) wide and 38cm (15in) deep.

STRUCTURE The house is built of painted wood and made to look like stucco. It has a flat roof, a first floor balcony and two sets of steps leading up to two front doors. From the front it could almost be a semi-detached house; from the open back it is clearly an individual house with one set of stairs.

LAYOUT OF ROOMS The house has two storeys with three rooms on each floor. On the ground floor there is a dining room with a staircase, a sitting room and a kitchen. Upstairs there is a landing (useful for storing the pushchair), a workroom and a bathroom.

KEY AND SCALE

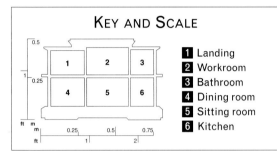

1	2	3
4	5	6

1 Landing
2 Workroom
3 Bathroom
4 Dining room
5 Sitting room
6 Kitchen

◁ Tubular steel was a favourite Bauhaus material and these chairs (actually made of brass with leather-covered tin seats) are very modernist for dolls' house furniture. The female doll has a Marlene Dietrich-style bob hairstyle and both dolls were made in Germany by Canzler & Hoffman.

▷ Sun tans were increasingly fashionable in the 1930s and they were often achieved by using sun lamps. This miniature sun lamp was produced in Germany in the 1930s, as were the gong and the jam pot set (all made slightly out of scale). These items were made to look as if they are made of chrome – a popular metal in the 1930s.

▽ The modernist style had roots in Cubism, reflected in this German wooden day bed. Its upholstery is in printed fabric.

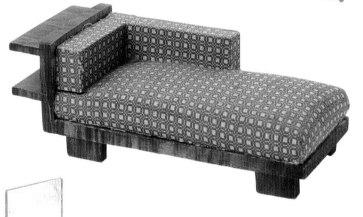

◁▽ The modernist period was a great one for bathrooms. This green marble bathroom set has a typically generous washbasin and wall-mounted mirror, although the bath is still Victorian in style.

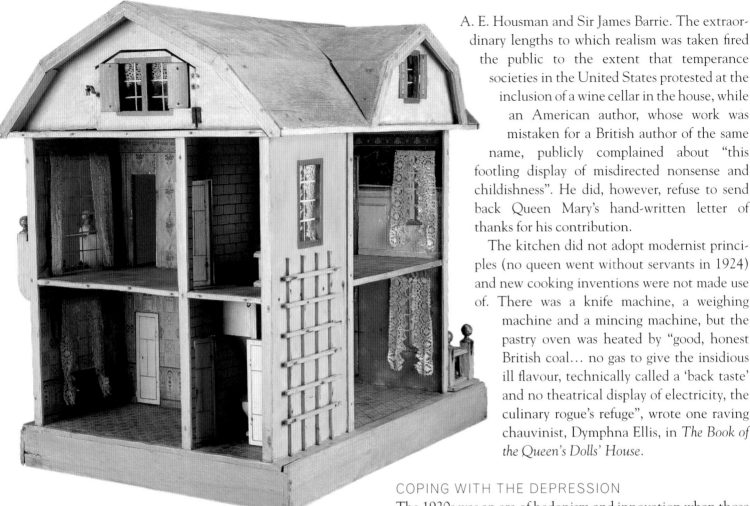

A. E. Housman and Sir James Barrie. The extraordinary lengths to which realism was taken fired the public to the extent that temperance societies in the United States protested at the inclusion of a wine cellar in the house, while an American author, whose work was mistaken for a British author of the same name, publicly complained about "this footling display of misdirected nonsense and childishness". He did, however, refuse to send back Queen Mary's hand-written letter of thanks for his contribution.

The kitchen did not adopt modernist principles (no queen went without servants in 1924) and new cooking inventions were not made use of. There was a knife machine, a weighing machine and a mincing machine, but the pastry oven was heated by "good, honest British coal... no gas to give the insidious ill flavour, technically called a 'back taste' and no theatrical display of electricity, the culinary rogue's refuge", wrote one raving chauvinist, Dymphna Ellis, in *The Book of the Queen's Dolls' House*.

COPING WITH THE DEPRESSION

The 1920s was an era of hedonism and innovation when those who had survived the First World War threw out all ideas associated with their elders who had got them into the mess in the first place. A decade later, following the Wall Street crash of 1929, the United States and Europe were in the grips of the Great Depression.

In one small corner of England, a village geared itself to help by designing dolls' house furniture to be made by the unemployed. Westacre Village Industries, Norfolk, was the brain

While modernism was the creed of the avant-garde, British craftsmen were creating Queen Mary's dolls' house which was given to her in 1924. Like the Stettheimer house (see page 139), real artists were commissioned for its design, from Sir Edwin Lutyens, the architect, and his garden collaborator, Gertrude Jekyll, to a whole series of authors who were asked to write tiny books for the library. They included Max Beerbohm,

△ This is a late red roof house made by Gottschalk (c.1930). It is unusual in that it has several open rooms, which allows more than one child to play at once. It has opening interior doors, and original floor coverings and wallpaper.

▷ During the Depression, Ysabel Birkbeck used unemployed boys, women and girls to make this Westacre furniture, copied from real English antiques. The bookcases, chests and bureaux were made of simple postcards, beads and pipecleaners.

◁ German pressed cardboard furniture with unusually bright printed "upholstery". The Little Red Riding Hood doll is made by the German makers Canzler & Hoffman (tradename Caho).

▽ Gottschalk went on making red roof houses after the First World War. This little house is probably one of their last houses and dates from c.1930. Its roses-round-the-door, lace-curtain style reveals the longing for security in this turbulent period.

child of Ysabel Birkbeck (see below left). She set unemployed women, boys and girls to work, with pipe cleaners, old postcards, beads, fabric and paint, to create copies of antique, mostly Queen Anne, furniture to sell to dolls' house owners. Others who taught included the vicar's wife and the school teacher. They were very ingenious, for example using painted lace, as canework chair seats. All pieces were painted to hide their origins, brown and black being the most common colours. Lord Roberts Workshops, also set up after the First World War to help disabled ex-servicemen, had jointed wooden dolls as one of its lines.

Britain was also indulging in an orgy of house building, creating the urban sprawl which we now accept around all our major cities. Four million homes were built between the two world wars and many of these were Tudor Revival, with rows of identical houses strung along main roads at one end of the scale and the grand Stockbroker Tudor house in its own large grounds at the other.

The style of the two decades between 1919 and 1939 is that seen on advertisements for Ovaltine: this is the period of the three-piece moquette suite, the flying ducks on the walls and the radiogram in the corner. Grander living rooms were panelled in dark oak and even the electric lights and fires were Elizabethan in style. Other typical features were an angularly cut mirror over the tiled fireplace and a standard light with a tasselled parchment shade. Such rooms are still to be found in suburbia, in museums about family life – and in dolls' houses.

Firms all over the world, at this period, were making toys for girls and boys, for this was an era which sentimentalized family life and childhood, as shown by the American paintings of small town family life by Norman Rockwell. Rosy-cheeked boys in little tweed shorts had their lead soldiers and Dinky toy cars; rosy-cheeked little girls in pinafore dresses had dolls' houses, dolls and furniture by Lines Brothers, three of the sons

▽ A chest of drawers, candlesticks and chair made by the American firm of Tynietoy (c.1930). Tynietoy furniture is easily identifiable as it is marked with the company's name and a dolls' house. The German doll dates from the 1920s.

△ The English firm of Tiny Toy (not to be confused with the American Tynietoy) made this evocative 1930s marbled gas cooker with surviving box. The toys were made by hand in London.

of the toymaker, Joseph Lines of G. & J. Lines. This firm had made rocking horses from the late 19th century and probably started to create dolls' houses around 1898 but, after the First World War, three of the sons of Joseph Lines – perhaps tired of his unwillingness to move forward – left the firm and set up on their own. Their company, Lines Brothers, originally used the tradename Triangtois; later changed to Tri-ang. By the mid-1920s they had a wide range of dolls' houses in modern styles but their best-known house arrived towards the end of the decade. It was the Stockbroker Tudor house, a realistic

miniature of the half-timbered neo-Tudor buildings rich stock-brokers were erecting all over the Home Counties in England.

Other makers at this time were the American company Tynietoy that produced idyllic sets of wooden furniture painted with flowers and, confusingly, the British firm, Tiny Toy. All were encouraged by the example of Princess Elizabeth who was given a child-sized play house in 1932, when she was seven. Y Bwthyn Bach, given by the people of Wales, had four rooms and was much copied, notably by Tri-ang (see page 140). Other firms produced posters and cut-out books about the house.

◁ The Liberace-style grand piano and music stool were made in the 1930s in the United States. Like many toys of the time, they are in cast metal.

△ The American firm, Tootsietoy, created this realistic set of kitchen equipment made of cast metal. There is a cooker, with side oven, a large dresser and an icebox.

△ Although it looks Georgian, this English house is in fact neo-Georgian and made around 1947 when the style was all the rage (look at post offices and town halls in England). It is a one-off, with an opaque glass ceiling that can be lit with electricity to cast a diffused light throughout.

WARTIME AND AFTER

This idealized vision of family life came to an abrupt end with the declaration of the Second World War in 1939; so too did European toy making. But in the United States it carried on although without great stylistic advances. In 1940, *Life* magazine reported on a southern Colonial dolls' house: "It has a great deal of charm, lights that light but lacks running water". But the house was finished with such realism that the cocktail glasses were pasted inside with faux cocktail cherries ready for Manhattans. The elegant lifestyle enjoyed by the dolls was reflected in its price of $98. Nearly every dolls' house now had a garage but houses in the modernist style were rare. One, said *Life*, "was very severely designed. It has glass brick walls, sun terrace, big expanse of horizontal windows." It cost, unfurnished, $25. The owner would have shared the problems experienced by new owners of real Modernist homes – the impossibility of furnishing them with anything other than expensive pieces of modern furniture.

One maker of the period was Bernard Ravca, a Russian who fled to Paris after the Russian Revolution and fortuitously found himself in the United States when war was declared. He had previously made large dolls but, during the war, he turned to dolls' house dolls, around 7cm (3in) high (see right).

One obvious change after 1945 was that the 1930s flat-roofed, Riviera house, distantly inspired by Le Corbusier, disappeared. In an era of deprivation, its leaks and rusty metal windows were impossible. Furthermore, no one who had experienced bombing or fighting anywhere in Europe was happy with wrap-around glass windows.

The Second World War affected civilians as never before, and the need for metal for ammunition, workers for war production and the isolation caused by a total shutdown of communications with the rest of Europe ensured that the British mass-production of anything as inessential as dolls' houses was phased out.

▽ Bernard Ravca made a living creating dolls' house dolls. This is a bridal set of groom, bride, priest and a little page who has the wedding ring on his cushion. They are made of crepe paper (c.1940s).

A STOCKBROKER TUDOR HOUSE

The original term was, in fact, "Stockbroker's Tudor" and was coined by Osbert Lancaster in 1938 in his book *Home Sweet Home,* along with other gems which now define inter-war style such as Bankers' Georgian and Vogue Regency. By the time he wrote the book, four million homes had been built in the suburbs of Britain – most of them in various versions of this style. From "accurate reproductions of Anne Hathaway's cottage, complete with central heating and a garage", the stockbrokers came from the green belt each day to the City of London.

Lancaster drew a telling little cartoon with his description. A chic lady sits in a four-poster bed, her breakfast tray on her lap. Behind her, huge ogee beams tie into the walls, a clearly wrought iron latch fastens the door and, on the wall, is a sampler and an early map of an English county. The 1930s dressing table sits in front of diamond-leaded windows. Nothing in this room is Tudor: the bed is Georgian, the latch bogus and the chintz hangings Victorian but, as Lancaster notes, they are "Tudor by adoption".

Although other countries have timber-frame buildings – Normandy in France is a prime example – they do not seem to have "revived" or, more particularly, produced an abundance of dolls' houses in the neo-Tudor style.

▷ Stockbroker Tudor style broke out in the Home Counties in the 1930s. This example, in a leafy Surrey glade, is replete with huge chimneys, lead-glazed windows and non-loadbearing beams, perfectly copied by Tri-ang.

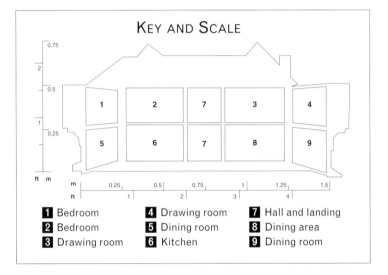

KEY AND SCALE

1	2	7	3	4
5	6	7	8	9

1 Bedroom   4 Drawing room   7 Hall and landing
2 Bedroom   5 Dining room   8 Dining area
3 Drawing room   6 Kitchen   9 Dining room

DATE Made by Tri-ang in the 1930s, this dolls' house was made in various sizes of which this is one of the largest.
SCALE 65cm (25½in) high, 120cm (47in) wide and 51cm (20in) deep.
STRUCTURE Wood with painted floors, metal frame windows and plywood applied as half-timbering.
LAYOUT OF ROOMS Four large rooms with central hall, stairs and landing. The bay windows and upper jettied floor within the two doors of the dolls' house contain further room space for a four-poster bed or easy chairs.

▷ The smart interior of the dolls' house tells a similar story to that of Osbert Lancaster's account of "Stockbroker's Tudor". Most of the furniture is reproduction of earlier styles, the exception is the record player and the kitchen equipment.

▷ Dolls' houses are generally very up-to-date on domestic equipment. These vacuum cleaners, upright and cylinder-type with attachments, were made by Taylor & Barrett.

△ Originally Knole sofas were made in the 17th century in Knole Park, Kent. They were highly popular in Stockbroker Tudor homes. This version is by Tri-ang. The dolls are German Caho dolls.

◁ The radiogram was the essential status symbol of the 1930s and took pride of place in the room. This one is in the first floor right-hand bay.

△ More period furniture from Tri-ang: a dining room set made to look like fumed oak. Table legs are bulbous, the upholstery pinned with brass nails. The tray is laid, apparently, with pewter.

RAMPANT CONSUMERISM

By the end of the Second World War, America had taken an inventive lead in domestic gadgets and shopping habits. The 1950s fantasy dolls' house was filled with the longed-for refrigerators, food mixers, washing machines, telephones and televisions even if real homes were not. Predictably, the European taste-formers were not in favour of American influences and tried to counteract the rampant consumerism with what became "Contemporary" style.

This was provided by Scandinavia, especially neutral Sweden which was seen as the epitome of caring modernity. Natural forms and materials were important – building bricks and wooden planks made bookshelves, curtains sprouted with spiky plant patterns such as thistles and cow parsley, and huge-leaved house plants like the Swiss Cheese and Mother-in-law's Tongue started to appear in room corners. The other feature of Contemporary style was the curious tapering legs on chairs and tables, finished with a ball to stop them digging into the carpet.

Science and technology, pushed on by the needs of the past war, was fully at work inventing new materials. Nylons were brought over by GIs but it was not until 1948 that the American designer, Charles Eames, created the first plastic chair. It seems that, unusually, dolls' house manufacturers had actually anticipated the real event, for, in March 1946, *Collier's Magazine* reported on "Toys for Tomorrow". This article mentioned a manufacturer of plastic dolls' house furniture "who expects to sell 150,000,000 pieces this year". The company had equipment for every room including a "model toilet with workable seat and seat cover, a Chippendale dressing table with an intricately carved mirror frame enclosing a real mirror, and a fireplace with andiron and legs". They sold

▷ This tiny German typewriter– copy of the real, stylish Olivetti – is made of cast metal and is a rare item for a dolls' house.

brilliantly and probably fulfilled his prophecy. What the makers of dolls' house furniture did not do was to make plastic furniture for its own sake, as Eames did. The medium was simply convenient, and it joined the long line of materials used in the past – wire, moulded metal, printed paper and cardboard – in faking real wooden furniture.

In general, dolls' houses lag behind real architecture and design; little girls in the 1950s were still playing with neo-Tudor houses furnished largely with neo-Georgian or Edwardian furniture, and with kitchens still an unhappy mixture of cook's domain and avant-garde units.

CHILDHOOD IDYLL

The 1950s, like the 1800s and 1930s, was a good time to be a child – at least if you were moderately wealthy and living in the West. By now, the vast majority of parents in the developed world could afford to buy their children toys. Unemployment was minimal, toys were inexpensive and children were indulged by parents who had themselves known hardship. Dolls' houses at this period tended to be small, portable and suitable in size for a small house, apartment or mobile home.

Fitting occupants for these dolls' houses were Grecon dolls. Grete Cohn (working as Grecon), who fled Germany for

◁ This English kitchen set dates from the 1950s. The sink has a plate rack, the solid table is typically English as is the kitchen cupboard with its sliding-door. The glass, dating from the 1870s, is German; the coffee pot, saucepans and plates are by Dol-Toi.

▷ This family of Grecon dolls is dressed in 1950s period style. Made by the German refugee, Grete Cohn, they are made of wire bound with wool and are full of charm.

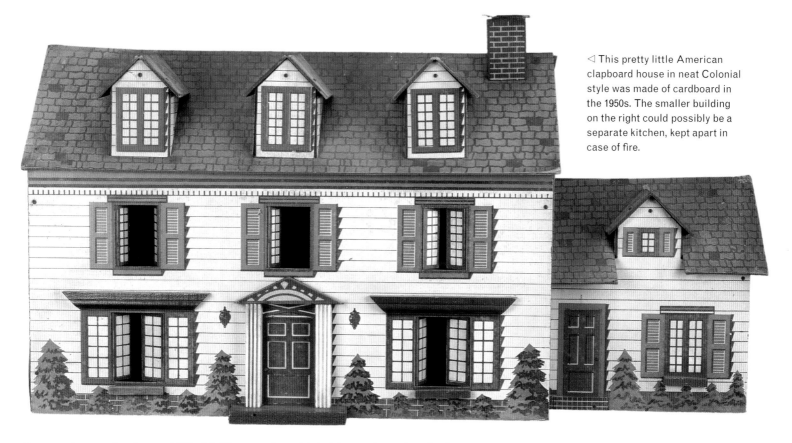

◁ This pretty little American clapboard house in neat Colonial style was made of cardboard in the 1950s. The smaller building on the right could possibly be a separate kitchen, kept apart in case of fire.

Britain during the Second World War, produced life-like and stylish dolls (see the family below). Grecon dolls had painted lively cloth faces and might be Red Cross nurses, naughty little boys or smart young mothers.

Children of the 1950s were carefully protected by their parents, perhaps in reaction to the War. The new world was summarized in the paintings of Norman Rockwell, whose highly realistic scenes of American life appeared regularly in the *Saturday Evening Post* until 1963. Fathers smoked pipes, mothers cheerfully cooked the greens and red-cheeked chil-

dren had swings in orchard trees. Teenagers had not quite been invented. In England, girls saw themselves as tomboyish and adventurous as Enid Blyton's *Famous Five* and yet still dreamt of owning their own mock Tudor dolls' house with a thatched roof and hollyhocks by the door.

A NEW TRADITION

The firms now extant were virtually all 20th-century companies which had few links with the past – the exception being Tri-ang, descendants of G. & J. Lines (see pages 145–6) whose first dolls' houses were made during the last years of the 19th century. In Britain, dolls' house makers included Amersham, Tudor Toys, Chad Valley and Marx, and their typical houses would measure between 45–58cm (18–23in) square. Mass-produced dolls' house furniture came from Dol-Toi, Spot-On by Tri-ang, and Taylor & Barrett. In the United States, source of some of the newest pieces of domestic equipment, Tynietoy and Renwal were the among the major makers. A great deal of plastic dolls' house furniture also came from Hong Kong, notably the Blue Box range.

The end of the Second World War saw the end of family servants in all but the richest homes, which, in turn, saw the invention of many domestic aids. Miniature versions of these started flooding from the United States, where modern kitchens were far in advance of Europe. The majority of families in the 1950s had neither television nor telephone and few had refrigerators – but the contents of dolls' houses were often in advance of real life.

△ More fake Tudor, although far less grandiose than the typical Stockbroker Tudor house. This English Tudor Toy version (c.1960) shows how traditional little girls are about architecture. The real style died after the War.

▽ Another English conservative little house by Chad Valley and made of tinplate. The bright interiors are more 1950s in style, with a heavy mangle and some neo-Georgian pieces by Kleeware, in plastic.

The Swedish firm of Lundby made dolls' houses and dolls' house furniture which epitomized the stylish 1960s and 1970s in Europe. If you need a quick reminder of what houses in this period were really like, Lundby will jog your memory (see opposite). They have large-patterned abstract wallpaper. The furniture and furnishings are particularly realistic too. Lundby made avocado bathroom fittings (see below right), including bath with shower attachment, bidet with towel holder and shelf, and even "his and hers" hand basins – for some extraordinary reason everyone's dream of luxury, which the dolls' house could fulfil. Otherwise, dolls' houses from the 1970s come in psychedelic combinations of purples and greens, influenced by such record covers of the time as *Yellow Submarine* by The Beatles and are made in printed paper, plastic and cardboard.

CHANGING TIMES

Although there are still examples of mass-produced dolls' houses, with furniture that might be found in real homes (Lundby houses are obvious examples), the 1960s marks the first decline of the dolls' house as a toy and indeed as a record of how people have lived – even Lundby has now closed down.

A possible explanation is that with the arrival of the teenager in the 1960s the real age of childhood became shorter and shorter. Young girls in the 1960s, 1970s and 1980s no longer wanted dolls' houses – they progressively wanted pop music, the latest fashionable clothes, and their own television and video. So, with a few notable exceptions, the toy-makers either retreated into the toddler market or provided the pre-teens with their needs.

One obvious exception is Barbie, made by Mattel in the United States, who is in fact not a dolls' house doll but, at 29cm (11½in) high, a proper doll for the 4–10-year-old age group. She was brilliantly conceived (in 1959) as the smartest girl around with a wardrobe to prove it and then she had to have her own house (see page 157). Mattel's Barbie houses have to be large in scale (to fit Barbie) and are made of sugary-coloured plastics, a sure sign that they are for young children with unsophisticated tastes. Their style is a sort of little girl's dream of Hollywood – the kind of house a film star like Jayne Mansfield would enjoy.

The German firm of Geobra Brandstätter makes plastic Playmobil toys. These include gingerbread Victorian mansions with their own dolls and furniture to add. The dolls are superbly made so that limbs are jointed and can be moved and pieces can be clipped together. Plastic, however, is not a particularly happy material for dolls' houses and dolls' house furniture. There have, therefore, been attempts to turn back to traditional materials for houses. For instance, printed tinplate dolls' houses were made in the 1980s by a company

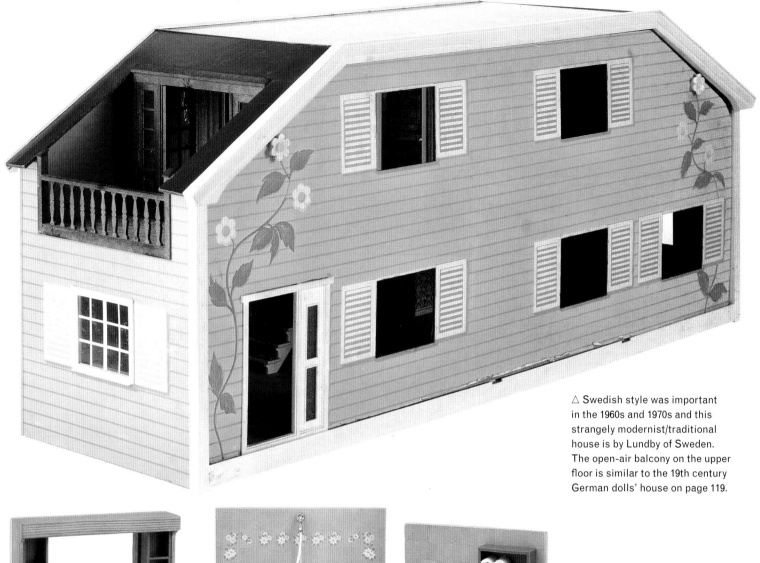

△ Swedish style was important in the 1960s and 1970s and this strangely modernist/traditional house is by Lundby of Sweden. The open-air balcony on the upper floor is similar to the 19th century German dolls' house on page 119.

◁ The avocado bathroom suite, so lusted after in the 1970s, got into dolls' houses too. By Lundby, this very smart room has his and hers basins, a bidet, flowered wall tiles and a shower.

called Today's Kids based in Arkansas in the United States. Printed cardboard houses have remained a constant.

GROWING ADULT HOBBY

At the other end of the scale there is a growing interest in dolls' houses among adults. The craft of making miniature houses and buildings in every conceivable style – from the Palace of Versailles to a Victorian shop – is one of the fastest growing hobbies among adults both in Europe and the United States.

These miniature houses and buildings can be made by craftsmen to order, or bought as kits from specialist suppliers. Furniture, fittings and accessories for the interiors are available from commercial firms, many of which can be painted and adapted to suit individual schemes. The most significant difference between miniatures and dolls' houses is scale; people interested in the miniature world like everything to be perfectly to scale whereas dolls' house enthusiasts do not worry about scale (as can be seen in many of the houses in this book).

NEW HOUSING

In 1976, an American architect, Ira Greenberg, designed a modern dolls' house for *Woman's Day* magazine and the preoccupations of the period are there (see below). The asymmetric house has picture windows and the kind of modernist look that the Bauhaus invented. It has spherical standard lamps, a games table and magazine rack in the drawing room, where the traditional three-piece suite is smartly angular in design. Macramé hangs on the walls and a houseplant sits in a white plastic tub on the floor. Outside there is a patio with more plants in white tubs, a table for *al fresco* eating and, yes, a barbecue. The objects are ingeniously made. Where firms like Westacre used the pipecleaners popular in the 1930s, Greenberg cuts pingpong balls, bottlecaps and toothpaste tops to make lampshades, handkerchiefs double as bedspreads and rugs, staples are handles and beads are knobs.

The post-Modernist architectural styles of the 1970s and 1980s gave rise to a new kind of domestic housing, even if it attended more to detail than basic structure – and its brightly coloured balconies, windows and door surrounds, its strange jokes and twists, can be seen in dolls' houses (such as the one

◁ Using psychedelic colours, post-Modernist patterning, this Polypops house could not be more 1970s. Made of cardboard and with paper furniture, it comes from England and is not particularly sturdy.

◁ Ira Greenburg designed this American house for *Woman's Day* magazine in 1976. It has an outdoor eating area, integral garage and quantities of split-level roofs. This style could only work in California.

△ Fisher Price created this set c.1980 following the American television programme *Sesame Street*. It is small-scale but politically correct. Hooper's Store, for instance, is bi-lingual in English and Spanish. The style is New York brownstone.

shown left) by firms like Polypops which created paper fantasies in such period colours as aubergine and purple and then added orange and olive green.

But that was the last detectable architectural style for new housing. Building today – for real families, that is – is almost all retrospective, whether it harks back to 1920s and 1930s minimalism and industrial buildings or whether it endlessly repeats the style of country cottages and 18th-century mansions. The only discernable changes are happening in huge public buildings like airports. And who would want their doll to play in an airport lounge?

MODERN TOY PRODUCTION

By the 1980s, toy production was moving to the Far East and becoming almost entirely plastic. The dolls' houses are starting to take on an air of real fantasy, fuelled perhaps by the Japanese cartoons which appear on computer games and off-peak television. Another type of 1980s dolls' house (shown at the top of page 156), which mixes the enjoyment of model making with

a history lesson about the late 19th century strives to be politically correct. An accompanying booklet describes the inhabitants of the house and then embarks on a story about the housemaid, her elder brother, wrongly imprisoned for petty theft, and the younger brother, 10-year-old George, who is cruelly thrown out of her employer's house as a guttersnipe. It certainly brings the period to life. Similarly, the American dolls' houses merchandized with the *Sesame Street* television programmes take care to embrace all races in their stories.

Unlike dolls' houses from even the 1930s, which fetch respectable sums at auction, post-1960s dolls' houses are fairly inexpensive and can be found in car boot sales, charity shops and flea markets. This is, therefore, an excellent area for new collectors.

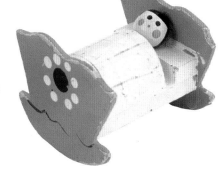

▷ This baby in a cradle comes from Erzegebirge, Germany and dates from the 1970s. It is made of painted wood and is virtually unchanged in style from 17th-century versions.

In the 1990s dolls' houses were no longer a series of little rooms where children could enjoy life in miniature, cook their own tiny scones and put their babies to bed; they had become true fairy-tale fantasies. Their intention was not to evoke adult life in a child's eyes but to flee from it into furry creatures, even fruit – just as computer games are set in a world of monsters.

In the 1950s, children played with dolls at the age of 12 or even older. In the 1980s and 1990s, the dolls' house market is confined to younger children. These children want fairy stories, bright colours, situations which have no connection with logic. They are not surprised when manufacturers suggest, and indeed provide them with, strawberry houses to live in and pigs that can fly.

THE FUTURE

Although there are many toy manufacturers producing plastic fantasy houses for very young children, there is also a growing market for traditional dolls' houses. Wooden kit houses can be bought in a wide range of styles and decorated or adapted to individual needs. Handmade houses are still being made and can be made to order. Many people enjoy amalgamating a dolls' house with their children's help. There are

△ Made by Marks and Spencer in 1983, this dolls' house is intended to be educational. Its accompanying book tells the story of the Victorian "family" who lived here with their servants – a cook-housekeeper, general maid and her 10-year-old brother. The interior is decorated in 19th-century style.

▷ The makers of Barbie, Mattel, created this rose-painted bedroom set, known as Littles, in heavy cast metal (c.1984). It was only made for a short period of time.

monthly dolls' house magazines, specialist shops and miniatures or dolls' house fairs are held regularly. Not only are traditional houses still available but also everything you could possibly need to furnish the house, including all the latest gadgets.

Throughout the centuries dolls' houses have appealed to both adults and children, and they still do. For adults they can create their own fantasies of, say, country house life in the 18th century. For children it is a chance for them to have a say in a world governed by grown-ups.

Enthusiasts all over the world are creating miniature houses in the same way as Petronella Dunois of Amsterdam in the late 17th century or Carrie Stettheimer in 1920s New York did. And in the same way as the King Street baby house replicates a real house in Kings Lynn, today there are craftsmen specializing in making dolls' houses based on people's homes.

While the current architectural style of dolls' houses is heavily influenced by the popular styles of the past, these houses will prove a fascinating record for future generations of how we lived, and dolls' houses will continue to enchant all age groups.

△ Dolls do not live in this Sylvanian Family house but anthropomorphic badgers, rabbits, mice and squirrels do. Well-made and designed, they were produced in Taiwan for a Japanese firm and sold through Tomy. They were first marketed in England in 1987 under the name of Woodbins.

▷ This is the place where Barbie lives. Made by her manufacturers, Mattel, the sugary pink and blue interior is pure Hollywood. It is made of plastic and dates from this decade.

Care, Restoration & Display

If you intend to become a dolls' house enthusiast you will find that the research and the collecting is the fun and the care and maintenance is the headache (unless you enjoy DIY). The problems of caring for full-size antiques is multiplied several times when the pieces are in miniature and difficult to handle. There are, however, so many dedicated collectors that new techniques and skills are constantly being developed.

Like all antiques, dolls' houses and their furniture should be kept in an atmosphere which is not too damp (fabrics and woodwork will rot) nor too dry (fragile wood will split); try to pick dry rooms which are not too fiercely heated and which are well ventilated. Entrance halls, landings and large corridors are good and, luckily, dolls' houses look good here too.

Dust, however, will be your major problem, so keep important pieces away from windows overlooking main roads and away from fires or boilers. In extreme circumstances they can be kept in soft bags – but that does seem a shame when dolls' houses were intended to be displayed and fussed over. Dusting should only be done with a fine soft brush or a tiny vacuum

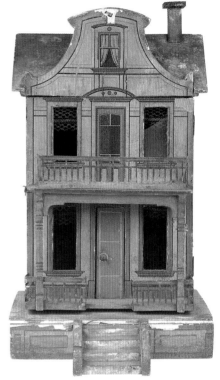

cleaner with fine muslin over its nozzle to catch any broken bits or pieces so tiny that they would disappear up the spout. Make sure, also, that the shell of the house is as dustproof as possible. Doors, windows, roofs and hinges should be as good a fit as can be made.

Next you have to worry about moth and woodworm. Worm will attack the soft wood of the house so keep checking that it is not infested. If you find tell-tale worm holes you can carefully treat the case with killer liquid – but, if in doubt, do consult a professional. Smaller pieces of furniture can be put in a plastic bag in the freezer for three weeks which generally kills the worm. If the wood is starting to crumble under attack, wax or resin can be injected to consolidate the damage but, again, do consult a professional before taking irrevocable action.

Moth is a great problem if your house has woollen carpets or upholstery so keep checking for signs. Moth killers that are intended to hang in clothes cupboards can be put to one side of the dolls' house and left undisturbed in a plastic bag for a week. The stillness of the air improves the effectiveness but make sure the moth killer is not in contact with the house.

When it comes to restoration the rule is *Don't*. The value of antique dolls' houses and their furniture lies in the originality of the condition, however distressed. Nearly all serious damage in old houses is caused by enthusiastic overpainting or tinkering. If restoration is essential always get the best advice before changing anything. Before that, take photographs of all the rooms and features from every angle so you have a record.

Because the skills involved in a furnished dolls' house are so many, you will have to think which restorer would be most suitable to the project. There are people who specialize in

◁ A red roof house from the 1930s (probably Gottschalk) with a paper base designed to be a pretty garden. Dolls' houses should not be restored without expert advice – which generally is to leave well alone.

▷ Large dolls' houses, even when unfurnished inside, make wonderful displays – but keep them in well-ventilated areas. This carpenter-made double-gabled house looks particularly good against the plain brick background of the room.

◁ This battered old blue roof house has missing sides so it will not stay upright. The original panelled base could be colour photo-copied to create new sides and the missing sections hand-painted in with water-colour. Damaged paperwork should be expertly treated.

▽ Gracie Cottage, was made from a wooden shoe-box by the 64-year-old hall porter of Greenwich Royal Infirmary, London in 1910. The matron asked him to create it for her daughter. The outside is painted with foxgloves, roses and cowparsley and the interior has hand-made furniture and paintings. It is displayed on a wooden plinth.

conserving fabric, paper, paints, furniture and dolls themselves. There are people who will be able to scrape off later paintwork with their fingernails to get back to the original but this, too, needs skill. If it seems a shame to own a charming dolls' house and not tinker with it, then buy a reproduction rather than an antique. This will have as many charming features as an original but will be yours freely to enjoy without affecting the value. You can even commission your own fantasy house like those 17th-century German and Dutch housewives and decorate to your taste.

Displaying your dolls' houses is fun. They look well in wide, empty spaces or in drawing rooms where they attract much attention. Large ones can stand on low bases and smaller ones on a side table at a good height for playing and viewing. But beware of vacuum cleaners crashing into their bases or of exposing your treasures to passing dogs or cats. But do not fall into the trap of treating them like museum exhibits. These are toys, they should look well used and played with. Putting them in glass cases is a great shame. If your collection becomes huge, then consider giving a room to them and displaying them on shelves in date or style order.

Where to See & Buy

Listed below are some of the most interesting museums and houses open to the public that have dolls' houses. Always telephone before visiting a museum to make sure their dolls' houses are on view, as well as to check opening times.
It is also worth asking the Tourist Information office in any town you may visit if there is a dolls' house in the local museum.

UNITED KINGDOM
Audley End House
Audley End
Safffron Waldon
Essex CB11 4JF

Bethnal Green Museum of
    Childhood
Cambridge Heath Road
London E2 9PA

Brighton Museum and Art Gallery
Church Street
Brighton
East Sussex BN1 1UE

Cambridge & County Folk
    Museum
2–3 Castle Street
Cambridge CB3 0AQ

The City Museum and Mappin
    Art Gallery
Western Park
Sheffield S10 2TP

Elizabethan House
Great Yarmouth Museums
4 South Key
Great Yarmouth NR30 2QH

Hereford & Worcester County
    Museum
Hartlebury Castle
Harletbury
Kidderminster DY11 7XZ

Hove Museum and Art Gallery
19 New Church Road
Hove
East Sussex BN3 4AB

The Estate Office
Longleat
Warminster
Wiltshire BA12 7NW

Museum of Childhood
42 High Street
Edinburgh EH1 1TG

Museum of London
London Wall
London EC2Y 5HN

Nostell Priory
Doncaster Road
Nostell
Nr. Wakefield WF4 1QE

Pollock's Toy Museum
1 Scala Street
London W1P 1LT

Town House Museum of Lynn Life
46 Queen Street
King's Lynn PE30 5DQ

Vivienne Greene Collection
The Rotunda, Grove House
Iffley Turn
Oxford OX4 4DU
(Always write beforehand to check times and conditions of opening.)

Uppark
South Harting
Petersfield
Hampshire GU31 5QR

Warwick Dolls' Museum
Oken House
Warwick
Warwickshire CV34 4BP

York Castle Museum
The Eye of York
York YO1 1RY

FRANCE
Musée des Arts Decoratifs
Department Jouets
Palais du Louvre
Paris
France

Musée National des Arts et Traditions
    Populaires
6 Avenue du Mahatma-Gandhi
F-75116
Paris

HOLLAND
Centraal Museum
Agnietenstraat 1
NL 3500 GC Utrecht

Frans Halsmuseum
P O Box 3365
2001 DJ Haarlem

Gemeetemuseum
Stadhouderslaan 41
25178 V The Hague

The Rijksmuseum
Stadhouderspade 42
1071 ZD Amsterdam

GERMANY
Germanisches Nationalmuseum
Kornmarkt 1
8500 Nuremberg

Münchner Stadtmuseum
St-Jakobs-Platz 1
D 8000 Munich

Museen der Stadt
Scholssplatz 1
521 Arnstadt

SWEDEN
Nordiska Museet
Djugardsvägen 6–16
11593 Stockholm

SWITZERLAND
Historisches Museum Basel
Barfüsserkirche
Steinenberg 4
CH 4051
Basle

USA
The Denver Art Museum
100 West 14th Avenue Parkway
Denver
Colorado 80204

Margaret Woodbury Strong
    Museum
1 Manhattan Square
Rochester
NY 14607

Museum of the City of
    New York
1220 Fifth Avenue
New York
NY 10029

Washington Dolls' House
    and Toy Museum
5236 44th Street N.W.
Washington DC 20015

Dolls' houses can be bought from auction houses, antique fairs, dolls' house and miniature fairs, specialist shops and occasionally from antique shops. They are also advertised in the collecting magazines – *International Dolls' House News,* Nexus Specialist Interest Publications, Nexus House, Boundary Way, Hemel Hempstead HP2 7ST and *Dolls' House World*, Ashdown Publishing Ltd, Shelley House 104 High Street, Steyning, West Sussex BN4 3RD. Houses that were made after the Second World War can sometimes be picked up at flea markets and car boot sales.

Listed below are a few of the major auction houses that specialize in dolls' houses.

UNITED KINGDOM
Bonham's (Chelsea)
65–69 Lots Road
London SW10 0RN

Christie's South Kensington
85 Old Brompton Road
London SW7 3LD

Phillips
Bayswater
10 Salem Road
London W2 4BU

Sotheby's
34–35 New Bond Street
London W1A 2AA

Sotheby's Sussex
Summers Place
Billingshurst
Sussex RH14 9ADx

Roseberry's
The Old Railway Station
Crystal Palace Station
London SE19 2AZ

Gray's Auction Rooms
34–36 Jamestown Road
Camden Town
London NW1 7BY

UNITED STATES
Cobbs Doll Auctions
1909 Harrison Road N
Johnstown
Ohio 43031-9539

Frasher's
Route 1
P O Box 142
Oak Grove
MO 64075

Mc Masters
P O Box 1755
Cambridge
Ohio 43725

Sotheby's
1334 York Avenue
New York
NY 10021

Skinner Inc
357 Main Street
Bolton
Massachusetts 01740

Therialts
P O Box 151
Annapolis
Maryland 21404

Withingtons
P O Box 440
Hillsborough
New Hampshire 03244

Glossary

Ashlar Masonry of large, flat blocks.

Baby house Name given to 18th-century English dolls' houses.

Baroque Heavily ornamental style of art and architecture from late 16th to early 18th century.

J. M. Barrie (1860–1937) Author of *Peter Pan*.

Bauhaus German school of functionalist and modernist architecture, founded in 1919.

Biedermeier Mid-19th century German decorative style noted for simplicity and use of pale woods such as ash, maple and cherrywood.

Bisque Porcelain, fired but not glazed.

Bonheur-du-jour A lady's small writing cabinet.

Box back Dolls' house with front opening and boxed back.

Pieter Breughel (1520–69) Flemish painter noted for satirical paintings of peasants.

Marcel Breuer (1902–81) Hungarian-born Bauhaus (see Bauhaus) designer noted for bent plywood and metal furniture.

Cabriole legs Chair legs made in the 18th century with upper convex curve and lower concave curve.

Chinoiserie Western adaptations of Oriental and Chinese designs and patterns.

Chromolithograph Coloured printing on stone or metal where illustration is not raised but made ink-receptive.

Tom Dixon Contemporary English designer.

Charles Eames (1907–78) American designer and architect, principally known for his swivel, leather chair.

Thomas Chippendale (1718–79) English cabinet maker using neo-classical and Rococo motifs.

Encorbelments An area of corbels (projecting stone blocks supporting architectural features on their top surface).

Garouste and Bonetti Living French interior designers using bright colours and fluid shapes.

Glazing bar A supporting bar for a glass window or door.

Groin The meeting of two stems of a cross vault.

Grödnertal A simple wooden doll made in the German region of Grödnertal.

Walter Gropius (1883–1969) German architect and designer, founder of Bauhaus (see Bauhaus).

Half-tester Bed with canopy supported at the head with no posts at the foot.

Jetty An overhanging upper floor.

Le Corbusier (1887–1965) Pseudonym of French modernist architect Charles Edouard Jeanneret.

Edwin Lutyens (1869–1944) English architect using classical and vernacular traditions.

Mansard roof A roof with two slopes on both sides and both ends, the lower slopes steeper than the upper.

Marquetry A pattern of inlaid veneers of various materials such as wood, brass and ivory – usually seen on furniture.

Mezzaluna A curved, two-handled herb chopper (literally a half moon).

Modernism A movement that created abstract, rectilinear architecture and design with loss of all ornament. Industrial motifs and modern materials were key.

Oeil du boeuf A circular or oval window (literally a bull's eye).

Parquetry Geometric pattern of different woods to cover floors or furniture.

Nigel Pawson Cult modern English minimalist architect and designer.

Piano nobile The principal storey of a classical house – usually on the first floor.

Post-Modernism An architectural style reacting to Modernism using brash, eclectic design.

Prefab A prefabricated building, especially those erected in Britain during the Second World War.

Psychedelic The decorative style of vivid colours and complex patterns associated with the altered perception caused by hallucinogenic drugs.

Quoin An external corner of a wall.

Rimpa A light and elegant Japanese style of the late 17th century.

Rococo Light 18th-century decorative style using much asymmetric ornament.

Norman Rockwell A 20th century American illustrator who uses a realistic style.

Jacques Emile Ruhlmann (1879–1933) French designer of luxury furniture in Art Deco, Moderne style.

Rustication Large blocks of ashlar (see Ashlar) left rough like rock.

Sabre leg A chair leg curved like a cavalry sabre tapering towards the floor.

Philippe Starck Cult French designer known for use of horn motifs and visual jokes.

Stockbroker Tudor Term for half-timbered domestic architecture built between the First and Second World War.

Tudorbethan Another word for Stockbroker Tudor.

Venetian window A window with three openings, the centre one arched.

Bibliography

DOLLS' HOUSE BOOKS

Desmonde, Kay, *Dolls – Dolls' Houses*, Charles Letts and Co Ltd, 1972

Earnshaw, Nora, *Collecting Dolls' Houses and Miniatures*, William Collins Sons & Co Ltd, 1989

Eaton, Faith, *The Ultimate Dolls' House Book*, Dorling Kindersley, 1994

Flick, Pauline, *The Dolls' House Book*, Collins, 1973

Forder, Nick, *Victorian Doll's Houses*, Apple Press, 1996

Jacobs, Flora Gill and Faurholt, Estrid, *A Book of Dolls and Doll Houses*, Charles E. Tuttle Company, 1967

Jacobs, Flora Gill, *A History of Dolls' Houses*, Cassell, 1954

Jacobs, Flora Gill, *Dolls' Houses in America*, Scribners, 1974

Glubok, Shirley, *Dolls' Houses*, Harper & Row, 1984

Greene, Vivien and Towner, Margaret, *The Vivienne Greene Dolls' House Collection*, Cassell, 1995

Green, Vivien, *English Dolls' Houses of the 18th and 19th Centuries*, Bell & Hyman, 1979

Green, Vivien, *Family Dolls' Houses*, G. Bell & Sons, 1973

Gröber, Karl, *Children's Toys of Bygone Days*, B. T. Batsford Ltd, 1928

Jackson, Valerie *Dolls' Houses and Miniatures*, John Murray Ltd, 1988

Jackson, Valerie, *Dolls' Houses: The Collector's Guide* Bison Books, 1994

King, Constance Eileen, *Dolls and Dolls' Houses*, Hamlyn, 1977

King, Constance Eileen, *The Collector's History of Dolls' Houses, Doll's House Dolls and Miniatures*, Robert Hale, 1983

Latham, Jean, *Dolls Houses*, A. & C. Black, 1969

O'Brien, Marian Maeve, *The Collectors' Guide to Doll Houses and Doll House Miniatures*, Hawthorn Books, 1974

Pasierbska, Halina, *Dolls' Houses*. Shire, 1991

Towner, Margaret, *Dolls' House Furniture*, Apple Press, 1993

Victoria & Albert Museum, London, *Dolls' Houses*, Her Majesty's Stationery Office, 1961, 1972, 1976

von Wilckens, Leonie *Mansions in Miniature*, The Viking Press, 1980

GENERAL

Childhood: an anthology Edited Penelope Hughes-Hallett, William Collins Sons & Co Ltd, 1988

Daiken, Leslie, *Children's Toys Throughout the Ages*, Spring Books, 1963

Country House Lighting 1660–1890, Temple Newsam Country House Studies 4, 1992

Playthings from the Past compiled by Geoff Egan, Catalogue for exhibition, Jonathan Horne, 1996

Calloway, Stephen, *Twentieth Century Decoration*, Weidenfeld & Nicolson, 1988

Cruickshank, Dan and Burton, Neil, *Life in the Georgian City*, Viking 1990

Davidson, Caroline, *The World of Mary Ellen Best*, Chatto, 1985

Durant, David N., *Living in the Past: an Insider's Social History of Historic Houses*, Aurum, 1988

Gelles, Edward, *Nursery Furniture*, Constable, 1982

Gilbert, Christopher and Wells-Cole, Anthony, *The Fashionable Fireplace 1660-1840*, Temple Newsam Country House Studies 2, 1985

Gilbert, Christopher, *English Vernacular Furniture: 1750–1900*, Yale, 1991

Gilbert, Christopher, Lomax, James and Wells-Cole, Anthony, *Country House Floors*, Temple Newsam Country House Studies 3, 1987

Godfrey, Elizabeth, *Home Life under the Stuarts*, Stanley Paul 1925

Kevill-Davies, Sally, *Yesterday's Children: the Antiques and History of Childcare*, Antique Collectors' Club, 1991

Praz, Mario, *An Illustrated History of Interior Decoration from Pompeii to Art Nouveau*, Thames and Hudson, 1964

Quennell, Marjorie and C. H. B, *A History of Everyday Things in England (series)*, Batsford, 1918 onwards

Scott Thomson, Gladys, *Life in a Noble Household 1641–1700*, Jonathan Cape, 1937

Taylor, Judy, Whalley, Joyce Irene, Stevenson Hobbs, Anne and Battrick, Elizabeth M., *Beatrix Potter, 1866-1943: The Artist and Her World*, The National Trust and Frederick Warne, 1987

Thornton, Peter, *Authentic Decor: The Domestic Interior 1620–1920*, Weidenfeld & Nicolson, 1984

Wells-Cole, Anthony, *Historic Paper Hangings* Temple Newsam Country House Studies 1, 1983

Index

Hitchcock, Alfred *128*, 157
Hoet, Gerard 31
Holland *18–23*, 19, 27, *27*, 30–2, *31–3*, 52, *52*, 53
Holly Trees house 75, *75*
Homans family 49
horses *29*
Housman, A.E. 144
Howitt, Mary 61

I
Industrial Revolution 110
Ingeborg, Princess of Denmark 88
Isle of Dogs 49
Italy *36*
The Ivies, Ashbourne, Derbyshire *58*

J
Jacobs, Flora Gill 6, 53, 94, 133
Japan *22*
Jekyll, Gertrude 144
Joy, Edmund 40
Joy, Mary Eliza 79–81
Jugendstil 109

K
Kensington Palace, London 36, 52
kettles, copper 91, *91*
Kihlberg, Emily 88, *88*
King, Constance Eileen 14, 67, 129
King Street baby house 50, *50–1*
King's Lynn 50, *50*
kit houses 132–3, *132*
kitchens *22*, 26–7, *29*, 46, 51, 62, *75*, *86*, *91*, 140, *146*, *150*
Kleeware *152*
Koferlin, Anna 15–16
Kress house 24, *24–5*, 27
Kress von Kressenstein family 25

L
lamps *77*, *113*
Lancaster, Osbert 148
Landfall House, Poole *136–7*
Lees-Milne, James *74*
Lehzen, Baroness 63
Lethieullier, Sarah 43
Life magazine 147
lighting
   chandeliers 16, 77, *122*
   electric 116
   lamps *77*, *113*
Lindner 67
Lines, G.& J. 11, 134, *134–5*, 146, 151
Lines Brothers *140*, 145
lithophanes *86*
London 70, 75, 88, 91, 101, 134, *134*
Lord Roberts Workshops *11*, 145
Lowell, James Russell 131
Lundby 152, 153, *153*
Lutyens, Sir Edwin 10, 144

M
Mackintosh, Charles Rennie *133*
McLoughlin Bros 8, *132*, 133
Magruder, Maddison *103*
maison de style 112, *112–13*
Manor House 96, *97*
mansard roofs *6–7*, *126*
Marks and Spencer *156*
Marx 151
Mary, Princess (daughter of George III) 56
Mary, Queen (consort of George V) 10, *110*, *140*, 144
Mary II, Queen 36
mass production 74, 96, 114
Massachusetts *72*
Mattel 152, *156*, 157
Mayhew, Henry 88, 90, 91
meat covers *122*
Michelham Priory dolls' house *138*
Mies van der Rohe, Ludwig 139
mirrors *113*
Mitchell, Bessie 94, *94*
Mock Tudor style see Tudor style

Modernism 138–41, 142, *142–3*, 147
Mompesson House, Salisbury 49
Mon Plaisir 36–7, *37*
Mondrian, Piet 139
Morris, William 133, 141
moth damage 158
Mrazek, Professor Dr Wilhelm 68
Musée des Arts Decoratifs, Paris 112
Museovirasto, Helsinki 130–1
Museum of London 49
Museum of the City of New York 68
music rooms 37
musical instruments *65*, *74*, *81*, *128*, *146*

N
Nationalmuseet, Copenhagen 88
neo-Georgian style *147*
neo-Tudor style *see* Tudor style
Netherlands *see* Holland
New York 64, 76, *76*, 139
New York *Daily Tribune* 128
New York mansion *82–7*, 83
New Zealand 131
Norfolk 98
Normandy 148
Norway 53
Norwich baby house 40–1, *40*
Nostell Priory baby house 48–9, *48*, 50
Nuremberg *14–17*, 15, 24, *25*, 28, *28*, 100
Nuremberg artisan's house 26, 28–30, *28–9*
nurseries *22*, *33*, 81, 94, 95

O
Oortman, Petronella 30, 32
Oortman house 30–2, *31–3*
open–air rooms *119*
Oranienburg 36, 52
Osborne, Isle of Wight 81

P
Paine, James 48, *48*
Palladian architecture 41, 43, 56, *58*, 76, *76*, 83

Palladio, Andrea 36, 49
paper, colour printing 100–1, *101*, 114, 128, *128–9*
Paris 141
Paris Exposition (1900) 125
"penny toys" *135*
"people dolls" *130*
Peter the Great, Tsar 10, 32
pets *86*, *113*
pewter 16, 101
Philadelphia 69, *69*, 91, 106
pianos *74*, *81*, *128*, *146*
pictures *19*, *77*, *113*
Pit-a-Pat 151
Pitts, Zasu *9*
plants *114*
plastic furniture 150, 152–3
plates *39*, *59*, *67*, *99*
Play People 152
policemen dolls 104, *104*
Polypops 154, *154*
porcelain *22*, 36, 52, *59*
Post-Modernism 154, *154*
poured-wax dolls 30
Princesses' house *60–1*, 61
printing, chromolithography 100–1, *101*, 114, 128, *128–9*
Psycho *128*, 157
pushchairs *122*

Q
Quantock house 40, 41
Queen Anne style *43*, *46*
Queen Mary's Dolls' House 144
Quennell, C.H.B. 95
Quennell, Marjorie 95
quilts *22*

R
radiograms *149*
Ravca, Bernard 147, *147*
Red Cross 131
"red roof" houses *117*, *144*, *145*, 158
Regency style 56, *58–9*, 63
Renaissance 8–9
restoration 158–9
Riehl, W.H. 66
Rietveld, Gerrit 139
Rijksmuseum, Amsterdam 19

Acknowledgments

The publishers would like to thank all those who provided pictures for this book or for allowing their pieces to be photographed.

KEY

t top; r right; l left; c centre; m middle; b bottom

IB Ian Booth; NN Nick Nicholson; ST Steve Tanner; TK Tim Knox; TR Tim Ridley; AAPL Architectural Association Picture Library; BAL Bridgeman Art Library; BMAG Bristol Museums & Art Gallery; CCHS Chester County Historical Society; CEM Colchester & Essex Museum; CFM Cambridge Folk Museum; CM Castle Museum Arnstadt, Germany; CM Centraal Museum, Utrecht; CSK Christies's South Kensington; CUK Corbis UK Ltd; CYM City of York Museums Service; Ed Edifice; EH English Heritage; EPC Elizabeth Prime Collection; FGM Reprinted with permission of the Florence Griswold Museum, Old Lyme CT; GN Germanisches Nationalmuseum; HGPC Hulton Getty Picture Collection; HM Historisches Museum, Basel; IA The Interior Archive, MI Mattel, Inc.; LMATD Lilliput Museum of Antique Dolls & Toys; LSC Laurence Scripps Collection, USA; MAD Musee des Arts Decoratifs, Paris; MAP Musee des Arts Populaire, Paris; MCDA Musei Civici D'Arte Antica; MCNY Museum of the City of New York; MOL Museum of London; GM Gemeente Museum; NM Nationalmuseet; NMS Nordiska Museet, Stockholm; NTPL National Trust Picture Library; RBPL Reed Books Picture Library; RHPL Robert Harding Picture Library; RIB Reed International Books Ltd; S Scope; SM Courtesy the Strong Museum, Rochester, New York; SMV Shelburne Museum, Vermont; SN Stadt Nurnberg; SPL Sotheby's Picture Library; V&A By Courtesy of the Trustees of the V&A; WDTHM Washington Dolls' House & Toy Museum; WDTM Warwick Doll & Toy Museum

Front cover RIB(EPC/TK); Back cover tl RIB(EPC/TK); tr, bl & br RIB.(ST); Front flap RIB (CFM/TR); Back flap RIB(CFM/TR); Spine RIB(IB); Front & back endpapers V&A; 1 RIB(EPC/TK); 2 RIB(IB); 3 RIB(EPC/TK); 5t RIB(TR); b RIB(TR); 6b RIB(ST); 6/7 NN (MAP); 7br RIB(ST), mbr RIB(ST); 8t CSK, bl RIB(ST), br NN(LSC); 9 SMV; 10 NN(WDTM); 11t RIB(IB), bl RIB(ST), b RIB(ST); 12 /13 background RHPL (Hans Nelsater); 13 NMS; 14 NN (GN); 15 NN (GN); 16 GN; 17t NN, bl NN, br NN; 18/23 RA; 19tl RHPL(Phil Robinson), tr RA, cl RA, cr RA, b RA, 20/21 RA; 22cr RA, tl RA, br RA, cl RA, bl RA, tc RA, c RA, tr RA; 24t NN(GN), b NN(GN); 25 NN(GN); 26 HM(Maurice Babey); 27 V&A; 28tl SN, br V&A, tr V&A; 29bl V&A, t V&A, br V&A, bc V&A; 30br NN, bl NN; 31 CM; 32b BAL(Hermitage, St Petersburg), t RA; 33cl RA, br RA, tr RA, tl RA, bc RA, c RA; 34/35 background AAPL(Simon Rae-Scott); 35 V&A; 36 MCDA; 37t NN (CMy), b NN (CM); 38t RIB(TR), br RIB(TR), bl NTPL(Bill Batten); 39cr RIB(TR), bl RIB(TR), tr RIB(TR), tl RIB(TR), br RIB(TR), mc RIB(TR), cb RIB(TR); 40l RIB, r RBPL; 41 CYM; 42 RIB(TR); 43tl HGPC, bl RIB(TR), tr RIB(TR), br RIB(TR); 44 RIB(TR); 45 RIB(TR); 46bcr RIB(TR), above cr RIB(TR), above cl RIB(TR), l of c RIB(TR), tr RIB(TR), bl RIB(TR), bcl RIB(TR), tl RIB(TR), br RIB(TR); 47 RIB(TR); 48 NTPL(Mark Fiennes); 49br NN (MOL), bl NN (MOL); 50tr RIB(TR), tl RIB(TR); 51bl RIB(TR), cr RIB(TR), br RIB(TR), t RIB(TR); 52 NN(GM); 53b NMS, below c NMS; 54 /55

background CUK(Eye Ubiquitous/Chris Bland); 55 V&A; 56 SPL; 57 RIB(TR); 58/59 EH; 58b EH; t Vince Ferry; 59bc EH, tr EH, cr EH, cbr EH, bl EH; 60 CSK; 60/61 CSK; 61b RIB(ST); 62/63 RIB(TR); 62b RIB(TR); 63t RIB(TR); 64tr CUK(Photo Images/Lee Snider), c MCNY; 64/65 MCNY(Gift of Mrs John W. G. Tenney and Mr Philip Milledoler Brett); 65tm MCNY, tl MCNY, mr MCNY, ml MCNY, br MCNY, tr MCNY, 66b CSK; 67tr RIB(ST), b RIB(ST), tl V&A; 68 MCNY(Gift of Captain Eppley); 69t CCHS, b CCHS; 70b Ed(Darley), t RIB(TR); 71t RIB(TR), bl RIB(TR), br RIB(TR); 72/73 RHPL; 73 RIB(EPC/TK); 74l RIB(TR), r RIB(ST); 75 CEM; 76l CUK(Photo Images/Lee Snider), r RIB(EPC/TK), bl RIB(EPC/TK); 77tr RIB(EPC/TK), bc RIB(EPC/TK), br RIB(EPC/TK), cr RIB(EPC/TK), tl RIB(EPC/TK), 78b CSK, t CSK; 79 CSK; 80b RIB(ST), t RIB(ST); 81 RIB(IB); 82 RIB(EPC/TK); 83bl CUK (Photo Images/Lee Snider), br RIB(EPC/TK), t RIB(EPC/TK); 84/85 RIB(EPC/TK); 86bc RIB(EPC/TK), tr RIB(EPC/TK), bl RIB(EPC/TK), ctr RIB(EPC/TK), ctl RIB(EPC/TK), tl RIB(EPC/TK), br RIB(EPC/TK), cl RIB(EPC/TK), mc RIB(EPC/TK); 87 RIB(EPC/TK); 88l CSK, r NMS; 89 NM; 90t CSK, b RIB(ST), lc RIB(ST); 91t RIB(ST); 92/93 CUK(Bettmann); 93 RIB(EPC/TK); 94 FGM; 95t CSK; 95b RIB(IB); 96t CSK, bl RIB(ST), br RIB(ST); 97t RIB; 98t BMAG, b RIB(TR), 99bc RIB(TR), cl RIB(TR), bl RIB(TR), t RIB(TR), br RIB(TR), cr RIB(TR); 100 CSK; 101b CSK, t RIB(ST); 102t CSK, b RIB(ST); 103b RIB(Rutherford B Hayes Library), t RIB(ST); 104b CUK(Ed/Philippa Lewis), t RIB(ST); 105tc RIB(ST), c RIB(ST), br RIB(ST), bc RIB(ST), tr RIB(ST), tl RIB(ST); 106/107 RIB(IB); 106l RIB(IB); 107t CSK, br RIB(ST), c RIB(ST); 108/109 S(Michel Guillard); 109 NN(MAP); 110t MOL, b WDHTM (By kind courtesy of Flora Gill Jacobs); 111 CSK; 112t Liz Garnett, b NN(MAD); 113b RIB(MAD/NN), t NN(MAD); 114br RIB(IB), br RIB(IB), bc RIB(ST), bl RIB(ST), cl RIB(ST); 115t RIB(IB), bl RIB(IB), bl RIB(IB), br RIB(ST); 116b RIB(ST), tc RIB(ST), tr RIB(ST); 117t RIB(CFM/TR), b RIB(ST); 118 RIB(EPC/TK); 119bl RHPL, br RIB(EPC/TK), t RIB(EPC/TK); 120/121 RIB(EPC/TK); 122mc RIB(EPC/TK), ml RIB(EPC/TK), tr RIB(EPC/TK), br RIB(EPC/TK), bl RIB(EPC/TK), tc RIB(EPC/TK), tl RIB(EPC/TK), mc RIB(EPC/TK), cl RIB(EPC/TK); 123 RIB(EPC/TK); 124tr NN, tl NN; 125 NN (MAD); 126tr Liz Garnett, br RIB(ST), tl RIB(ST); 127ml RIB(ST), mr RIB(ST), br RIB(ST), bl RIB(ST), t RIB(ST), mc RIB(ST); 128b RIB(ST), t Courtesy SM, Rochester, New York; 129 tl RIB(ST), tr NN; 130tr CSK, tl RIB(Kenn Skrupky); 131t CSK; 132b RIB(ST); 132c RIB(ST), t NN(MAD, Paris); 133 CSK; 134b Nicholas Kane, t RIB(ST); 135tr RIB(ST), tl RIB(ST), bl RIB(ST), tm RIB(ST), cm RIB(ST), br RIB(ST); 136/137 background RIB; 137 NN(LMADT); 138 RIB(Michelham Priory, Sussex); 139t MCNY(Gift of Miss Ettie Stettheimer); 140t RIB(TR), b RIB(TR); 140/141 RIB(ST); 141b CSK, t RIB(ST); 142tl CUK (Ed/Philippa Lewis), tr RIB(TR); 142/143 RIB(TR); 143tr RIB(TR), cb RIB(TR), b RIB(TR), c RIB(TR); 144b CSK, t CSK; 145b RIB(TR), t RIB(ST); 146tl RIB(ST), tr RIB(ST), bl RIB(ST), b RIB(ST); 147t RIB(IB), b RIB(ST); 148t AAPL(H. Cook), b RIB(TR); 148/149 RIB(TR); 149cl RIB(TR), tl RIB(TR), cr RIB(TR), tr RIB(TR); 152t RIB(ST), b RIB(ST); 150t RIB(ST), b RIB(ST); 151t Christies Images, b RIB(ST); 153b RIB(ST), t RIB(ST); 154t RIB(ST), b MCNY(Gift of *Woman's Day magazine*); 155b RIB(ST), t RIB(ST); 156b RIB(ST), t RIB(ST); 157b MI(Barbie is a trademark owned by and used under license from MI. Copyr 1997 MI. All Rs Reserved.), t RIB(ST); 158t RIB(IB), b RIB(ST); 159b CSK, tl A (Schulenburg); 164b RIB(IB), t RIB(IB); 165b RIB(IB), t RIB(ST); 166t RIB(IB), b RIB(IB); 167t RIB(IB), b RIB(ST)

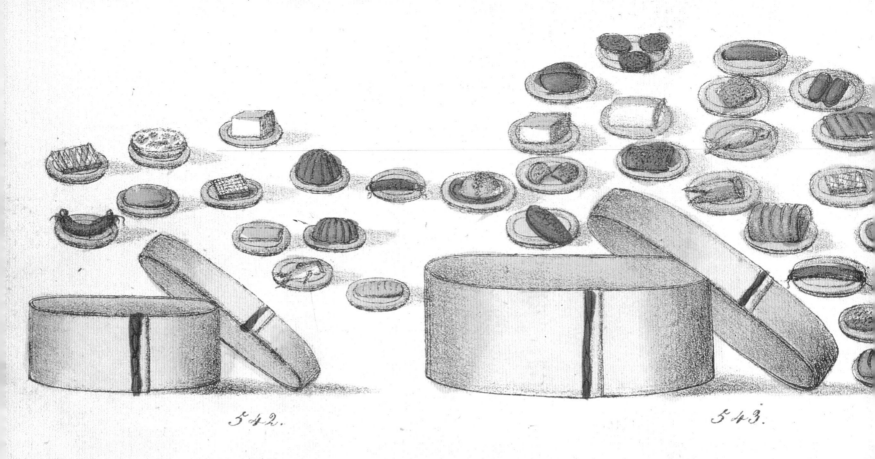

542.   543.

546.   547.